❧ Homeschooling Our Children ❧
Unschooling Ourselves

Homeschooling Our Children Unschooling Ourselves

by Alison McKee

Bittersweet House
Madison

ISBN 0-9657806-2-7
Printed in the United States of America
Book design by John Townsend
Back cover photo by James Gill

Library of Congress Cataloging-in-Publication Data

McKee, Alison.
     Homeschooling our children : unschooling ourselves /
by Alison McKee. — 1st ed.
     p. cm.
     Includes index.
     ISBN 0-9657806-2-7

     1. Home schooling. 2. Home schooling—United States
—Curricula. 3. Curriculum planning—United States.
I. Title.

LC40.M35 2001   371.04'2
                                 QBI01-700583

≈ Table of Contents ≈

Foreword

THIS BOOK IS ABOUT HOW WE DECIDED TO HOMESCHOOL our children and what happened when we did. We started our homeschooling adventure in 1983, when our son was five, and we soon became active in the then-budding homeschooling movement. So it was with some surprise when, in 1992 — as I was deciding to return to part-time teaching so that my husband, David, could pursue an advanced degree — many of my friends, family, fellow teachers and homeschoolers asked if we were now going to enroll our children in school.

Given our commitment to and support of homeschooling over the years, this question surprised me — and made me wonder: did people really understand what we were trying to do? This was what motivated me to write this book. I hoped that telling the story of our homeschooling experience would reveal how homeschooling — initially thought of as an educational choice — often becomes a life-style choice. Families that decide to let their children learn in a home setting rather than a school setting often discover what we discovered — that children easily and naturally become integrated with their community, and that by learning together, the family benefits in extraordinary and unexpected ways.

Many times on our homeschooling journey I had to remind myself to let my children "show me the way." I offer this book in the hope that it can help show you the way.

(Readers, please note that although the events described in this book are real, in some instances the names of students, teachers, and acquaintances have been changed.)

Acknowledgments

THIS BOOK COULD NEVER HAVE BEEN COMPLETED without the love and caring support of many people. The enthusiasm of my dear sister, Janet Thompson Henningsen, who read the initial draft and has supported my efforts throughout, gave me the courage to continue. Others in my homeschooling circle of friends, at home and across the country – including the hundreds who have called to ask about homeschooling – have helped clarify and give voice to our evolving educational philosophy. I thank you for your ideas and your kindness.

When we moved to Madison, Wisconsin, I helped found a support group for homeschoolers, "Home-Oriented Meaningful Education" (HOME). This group, which now numbers more than one hundred families, has been the backbone of support that has shared the joys of homeschooling and kept us going in times of discouragement. Thank you all for being there. And special thanks for their special support to these homeschoolers: Camy Matthay, Daria Northway, Donna Mahr, Susan Horein, Emily Bourne, Grace Llewellyn, and Melanie Sax.

To our friends whose experiences I have drawn upon for this book, I also owe thanks: Becca Patterson, Elena Reyes, John Williams, Roger Hurd, Matt Hogan, Sophie Zermuehlen, and Vern Haubrich.

I also wish to thank my editor and book designer, John Townsend, who has known us since before our children were born. John, your insights and skills have transformed my story into the book that I had hoped it would be; without your efforts this book would not be.

Of course, I want to thank my partner in life, David McKee, who began this journey with me by simply listening and being open to my then-radical notions about keeping our children out of school. Over the years, you have been my mentor, my sounding board, my conscience, my guide, my love. Thank you, David, from the bottom of my heart.

And finally, my profoundest thanks go to our children, Christian and Georgina. *Homeschooling Our Children, Unschooling Ourselves* (a title contributed by Georgina) could not have been written without your participation and loving support. To you, I offer my deepest love and gratitude – you have truly "shown me the way."

Alison McKee
Madison, Wisconsin

⚜ Introduction ⚜

Why Am I Telling My Story?

For many of us, home-based education bears absolutely no resemblance to what goes on in schools.... Our real work is not about academics, it is about living.
    — Earl Stevens, Home Education Magazine, *May/June 1993*

WRITING AN AUTOBIOGRAPHY is a rather presumptuous undertaking. It assumes that the author has an interesting life story to tell — and that the public is interested in that life. Often the autobiographies we read are of people already famous or people who have done remarkable things in their lifetimes. I have no such credentials. I am simply a mother who has spent the last seventeen years homeschooling my two children.

So why do I want to tell my story?

My primary reason for inviting you into our home and sharing our homeschooling experience with you is because I believe many people — homeschooling families, teachers, and anyone who has been traditionally educated — might gain insight into their own learning experience by reading our story. My hope is that with a better understanding of how children really learn, we might all be inspired to take on issues of educational reform and work together to create better educational opportunities for all of our children.

Our family came to choose homeschooling not because it offered us an opportunity to protect our children from social ills, or to provide them with an education (religious or otherwise) superior to that offered by either public or private schools. Rather, we chose homeschooling because it offered us the opportunity to let our children continue to be the creative and enthusiastic children they were from the start. We believed that our children wanted to live as they had in their preschool years: free of someone else's notions of what was important to learn, and when to learn it. For these reasons, we turned to homeschooling as the only means by which we might preserve, for our son, Christian, and our daughter, Georgina, the natural gift that they and all children are born with: an insatiable appetite for learning.

How did we come to possess such ideals? My husband, David, and I are children of the '60s — a time when many schools were experimenting with alternatives to traditional curricula and methods. Although neither of us attended such schools, our college experience at the University of Pacific's Raymond College was less traditional than most. Like other incoming students, we were sent a "summer reading list" with suggested reading material. That list included books written by both A.S. Neill and John Holt, who were known for their radical views of education and who had unique perspectives on the lives of children. Neill and Holt were educators who proposed radical educational reform long before it became a classroom topic. In that summer of 1969, before David and I had met, we simply read the books on our reading lists, and that fall we came to Raymond College to begin our studies. How ironic that our summer reading material, largely forgotten, would become so important much later in our lives.

Who were A.S. Neill and John Holt, and what had they done to be considered radical educators with unique perspectives on the lives of children? Both men were part of the progressive movement in education, a movement that began in the early part of the twentieth century. "Progressive" educators believed that using external rewards and punishments to teach children was artificial and wrong. They turned their efforts toward reinforcing the natural curiosity of children to learn about their world. Since its debut, this progressive movement has been both hailed as the best and ridiculed as the worst way to educate children. Over time, many "progressive educators" lost their focus and returned to using coercion and persuasion to teach their students, and thus the movement failed. Neill and Holt, however, remained committed to the ideals of progressivism.

In 1921, A.S. Neill founded Summerhill, a progressive school located in Suffolk, England. Neill believed that all children are born with an innate sense of goodness and the potential to love. He established Summerhill as a school that strived to nurture these innate characteristics by giving students freedom to learn as they chose to learn. He sincerely believed that the aim of education was not so much to teach as it was to help children learn with joy — and to find happiness in life. He wanted Summerhill to be a school where children were given opportunity to develop emotionally as well as intellectually. According to Neill, children would not have a healthy emotional development if coercion, punishment or force were used on them; he forbade such methods at Summerhill. Staff and students at the school were held to the highest standards of respect for the individual. Summerhill became an internationally famous school and, in time, other schools tried to emulate it.

John Holt held similar beliefs. He was an American educator with extensive "front line" experience in traditional as well as alternative schools. He became known to the general public when he published *How Children Fail* in 1964. This book discussed how schools hinder children's inborn desire to learn, and asked educators to look at their teaching methods, rather than blame students for such failures. In 1967, Holt published *How Children Learn,* in which he described how children's failure to learn can be overcome if educators were simply willing to adapt their methods to the natural learning style that each child possesses. Both of these books were based on the sensitive and insightful observations Holt had made while teaching in schools in Colorado and Massachusetts. These two books — and Holt's work in university settings, on the lecture circuit, and in his prolific writing — caused quite a stir among those who felt that traditional forms of education were the only means by which children could learn. His writing was dedicated to advocating change in the way we think about children and learning. Like Neill, Holt believed that children are the best directors of their education and, given a helping hand, without coercion, would naturally develop into well-adjusted and competent adults. This idea came to be known as "unschooling." By the time of his death in 1985, Holt had a national reputation as an advocate of "homeschooling through unschooling."

The ideals of these two men, in conjunction with David's and my observations of the world of traditional schooling, opened our minds to thoughts of trying to provide Christian and Georgina with an unschooled life. In the fall of 1983, when Christian was five, we took the plunge and kept our son home from school. I think of that time as stepping into an abyss, because there were so few resources available for unschoolers. Holt's books had been published, his newsletter, *Growing Without Schooling,* was in its fifth year, and Clonlara, a small school in Michigan, offered advice and administrative support to families wishing to homeschool. Aside from these few resources, David and I didn't have a large support network — although within a year, Nancy Wallace had published *Better Than School* and soon after that *Home Education Magazine* began publication.

As these writers and advocates of unschooling began to step forward, some Christian families — many of whom were following the wise and generous leadership of Dr. Raymond and Dorothy Moore — also began to turn to homeschooling to provide their children with religiously-based instruction unavailable in public schools, and unaffordable or inappropriate in parochial schools. Within a short time, homeschooling had gained a strong Christian voice, and a market for curriculum, correspondence schools, standardized tests and the like had sprung up across the country. This larger Christian-oriented voice, quite traditional in tone and methods, overshadowed the smaller yet persistent voice of unschoolers like ourselves who viewed homeschooling not merely as adopting traditional schooling practices for use in the home, but as a real departure from traditional schooling methods.

When parents ask David and me about homeschooling, we are generally asked about curriculum, achievement testing, knowing what to teach when, socialization, and how one goes about getting homeschooled children into college. It is common for such questions to come on the heels of comments such as, "I could never do that," "I wouldn't know what or how to teach," or even, "Your children must be self-motivated learners." These questions and comments are not "wrong"; they simply reflect the "facts" traditional schooling has taught: that curriculum is important because "it" knows what children need to know and when; that achievement testing is the only way to assess whether or not a child is successful; that schools are the only places children learn socialization skills; that college is the ultimate goal for anyone wishing to be successful in this world; that children will not learn anything unless they are *made* to study; that teaching is a highly-skilled profession that takes years of training to master; and that only "gifted" children enjoy and pursue learning with any sort of vigor. For those of us who grew up attending traditional schools, these are bedrock beliefs. Yet living a life unencumbered by such assumptions has been the motivating factor for a small minority of families who choose the homeschooling path. It is an alternative that allows us the opportunity to give our children a life rich in experience and free of confining "professional" attitudes about what children must learn in order to succeed.

What is the unschooler's life like? How is unschooling accomplished? How does it compare with traditional school experiences? These are serious questions David and I have asked ourselves for years, and as our children — who are now teenagers — launch themselves into the "real world," we have come to understand that the answers to these questions have always been at our fingertips, but obscured from view because of our traditional educational experiences. The years since 1983, when we bravely decided to homeschool Christian and Georgina, have been filled with struggle and pain simply because we had to find our own way; and yet the joys and triumphs have been greater than we could ever have imagined. Over the years, I have come to believe that anyone might experience the successes we have experienced with our children. It simply takes being open to the lives our children wish to live, and learning to trust in and nurture the inner voice that each child is born with. Our story is offered in hopes that readers will be encouraged to take the risk of listening to the inner voice of their children and allow them the freedom to follow it.

Unschooling has offered me more joy than I had imagined possible, and I believe others might find such joy if they dare to follow the amazing dreams of their children.

⁓ Chapter 1 ⁓

I Want To Become A Teacher

Most children in school fail. Why do they fail? They fail because they are afraid, bored, and confused.

— John Holt, How Children Fail

WHEN I WAS IN THE FOURTH GRADE, I'd spent two weeks learning the skills of long division and still I was confused about when to insert a zero in the quotient. Now I was faced with my first test and there was the problem staring back at me: divide 7440 by 24. The first step was easy: simply use 2 as my trial divisor and begin estimating the quotient. Not being terribly adept at such estimations, I began by choosing the quotient of 2 and then debated whether it should go above the 7 or the 4 in the dividend. "Whoops, I almost forgot — I'd better do some multiplying to test my estimation before I get carried away. Let's see: 2 x 24 is 48. Too much left over. 3 x 24 is 72. Much better." I think to myself, maybe this problem will be easy; one without zeros in the quotient.

As I faced the next step, I realized that maybe I'd been doing a bit of wishful thinking because here I was, once again, having to consider whether or not I needed a zero in my quotient. As I mulled the question over and tried to remember all the rules about when to bring down, when to use a zero as a place holder, and where, in heaven's name, to place each digit of the quotient so that it sat in proper relation to the dividend, my mind drifted off. What's the point of all of this anyway? Besides being boring and tedious, I saw no immediate need to learn this. Obviously, there had to be another, different way to do the work without having to remember all these intricate steps. As I lost myself in those all-too-familiar thoughts, I gazed out the window at the eucalyptus grove outside the window. I wanted to go outside and walk the paths with the people who frequently passed by with dogs or small children.

Suddenly, my teacher's voice drew me out of my reverie: "There's ten more minutes left before recess, class. Those of you who are done can bring your tests forward and then find something to read until the bell rings. The rest of you continue working until the bell." That settled it. Time to refocus, get done and out to recess. As I returned to my work, I realized I'd begun to daydream while trying to figure out whether or not I needed to add a zero to my quotient. Reluctantly, I placed a zero in the quotient. Even though I was unsure about whether or not it was needed, there was one thing that became crystal clear: I wanted to become a teacher so that I could find different, more exciting ways to help children learn. I knew there had to be better alternatives for learning than hours of drill work, pages of homework, and tests given on days when it would be much better to be outside exploring.

Tim and the milk horse

Although the memory of that school math test has remained with me all of these years, my fondest memories of learning had little to do with my school experiences and much more to do with what I managed to learn on my own. I grew up in San Francisco in the 1950s and 1960s as the middle child in a family of four girls and a boy. My father was a physician and my mother, although college-educated, chose to stay at home with us. It was at her side that I learned about what fascinated me most then and since: the world of those who were blind.

My mother had worked at The Perkins School for the Blind in Watertown, Massachusetts, before her marriage. She shared many stories with us about what it was like to work with blind children. One of them was Tim, a young boy at the school with whom Mom had developed a special relationship. I loved to hear her story about "Tim and the Milk Horse."

Tim was a young kindergarten student when I first met him. One morning during recess, Tim heard the horse-drawn milk cart clatter onto the school grounds and asked me what it was. When I explained that it was the milkman, Mr. Parker, and his horse, May, Tim said, "Oh, I love horses."

I asked, "Would you like to see Mr. Parker's horse, Tim?"

"Yes, please, Miss Cairns."

"Hold my hand and come along, then."

Mr. Parker was unloading milk when Tim and I walked up to the delivery wagon. I asked, "Mr. Parker, may Tim see your horse?"

"Of course! Bring Tim over here and I'll lift him up so he can pet her."
Tim and I walked around to the horse.

"Tim, this is my horse. Have you ever seen a horse?" In hushed tones
Tim answered, "Not a real one."

Mr. Parker continued, "May is a very gentle horse, just pet her right
here," and he put Tim's hand on May's neck. Then Tim began to explore
the rest of the horse. He patted her all over. When Mr. Parker put Tim
down, he came back to me. "Miss Cairns," he said, "Mr. Parker's horse is
old. She's so old, she'll die soon."

"What makes you think so, Tim?"

"She's so big!"

Mom explained to us that Tim's experience of horses was that of
rocking horses and toy horses — so he believed that all horses were small!
When he felt May and learned how large she was, he thought, as many
young children do, that her size indicated her age. Tim believed that
surely a horse as big as May must be very, very old!

Mom told us other fascinating stories from her days at The Perkins
School. If, for example, we were unwilling to try a new dish that she was
serving for dinner, Mom might remind us of our manners by talking
about the children at Perkins.

"When I was at Perkins, complaints about the meals were not allowed until the food had been tasted. Do you remember why?" (In a mono-
tone, we'd chime in, "Yes, Mom," in hopes that she wouldn't repeat the
story for the umpteenth time.)

"You know, at Perkins all the children were blind. This meant that
they never complained about a meal before tasting it, because its appearance didn't bother them. Sometimes the children might complain about
the smell of a dish, but the rule was that they must taste each dish before
refusing to eat it. In our home the rules are the same, so please taste this
meal before you complain about it."

Many similar stories piqued my interest about what it must be like
to work with blind children.

I want to become a teacher of the blind

It didn't take much to turn my budding interest in working with
blind children into a full-fledged ambition. In 1958, our family went
back east to visit Mom's family. We planned a vacation that included
visits with our many aunts, uncles, and cousins and, of course, lots of
sightseeing. One of these trips was to The Perkins School. At Perkins, we

visited Dr. Gabriel Farrel, a dear friend of Mom's. Dr. Farrel took the whole family on a tour of the Perkins campus. I was instantly enthralled. There was a history museum especially designed for use by blind students. In the museum, there was a collection of stuffed wild animals that could be removed from their display cases and held by the children. In the main hall of the school stood a huge globe of the world in relief. The five of us Thompson children were encouraged to hold hands and encircle its circumference to determine how big it really was. Outside, there were sandpaper-like patches inlaid in the sidewalks. The students would use these patches as auditory and tactual cues for traveling on the campus grounds. After our personal tour was over, we went back to Dr. Farrel's office and were given braille alphabet cards as souvenirs of our visit. I treasured mine for many years.

Treasures in the attic

That visit and the stories my mother had told me about Perkins infused me with a strong desire to teach blind children. I was drawn by the magical quality of the school and a longing to be the next Anne Sullivan for a yet-to-be-found Helen Keller. (Anne Sullivan, Helen's teacher, had originally come from Perkins.)

When we returned home from our vacation, Mom became my touchstone to the new world I had discovered at Perkins. She continued telling me stories about her life at Perkins, but most importantly, she shared with me her collection of personal treasures she'd kept from her days there. Most significant was a signed photograph of Helen Keller, which bore the inscription:

"To Janet Holloway Cairns, with fragrant memories of a glorious day in Honolulu. Helen Keller, December 1937."

Besides that photograph, there was a slate and stylus (a hand-held writing board and a stylus used to write braille) and some old "Moon Type" books. If I promised to be careful, Mom allowed me to play with the slate and stylus. Without real braille paper, my attempts to write braille were rather futile, but I didn't mind. Just making holes in paper was a satisfactory substitute for being able write real braille. If working with the slate and stylus didn't interest me, I'd read the Moon Type books. "Moon Type" is embossed printing embedded into the back side of the page so that its relief may be read on the front of each page. These books were huge and the pages had turned yellow with age; I loved to look at them and dream about a time when I'd use slate and stylus and braille books to teach *my* students.

Over the years, such memories as my failed long division test, or those days when my Mother spoke to me of Perkins, or the time I spent in our attic with slate, stylus and Moon Type books, fueled my desire to become an exceptional teacher of blind and visually impaired children.

Germain

Years later, as a veteran teacher at age thirty, I was facing failure. My experience with Germain became a turning point in my life. Germain had become my student when he was four years old and enrolled in a private preschool. He was a bright child filled with curiosity about the world around him. He wanted to know about everybody and everything. When I first met him, he asked me who I was, why I was there, and what I would do with him. He was articulate, had a large vocabulary, and talked easily with me, a total stranger. By the end of my initial visit, I was impressed. He was clearly bright and eager to learn.

As a teacher of visually impaired children, my task was twofold: to teach Germain the skills he needed to participate in his preschool class, and to make an assessment of his functional vision; that is, how he actually used his vision. This, in turn, would help me determine whether Germain should read braille or large type.

Initially, Germain and I got along marvelously. My first lesson plans focused on movement activities, creative play, and games that taught basic concepts. I took advantage of his creativity, his curiosity and physical energy, and was able to teach him, using his interests as the springboard for my lessons. For example, when he was interested in making himself a necklace of large colored beads, I taught him the names of the colors he could see. Since he seemed to enjoy identifying colors, we created a game of cards based on color identification tasks. Building with blocks and Duplo Legos was one of his favorite things to do. I took advantage of this interest and reinforced his color identification skills, while at the same time introducing him to number and shape concepts. Using Fisher-Price and Lego figures as part of our building games, it was easy to teach Germain concepts of spatial relationship while continuing to reinforce color and number concepts.

Unfortunately, my opportunity to offer such lessons was limited. Germain was required to learn particular skills in order to meet the demands of his preschool curriculum. Soon I found myself having to forego lessons that took advantage of his unique interests and adjust my educational goals to fit those of the preschool curriculum. When Mrs. Blaire, his preschool teacher, was required to teach reading readiness skills, I was required to pre-teach Germain those same lessons (using braille and large type). This would enable him to participate in the regular classroom work the following day; but Germain was very unhappy with this change because, at the time, he had little interest in learning to read.

I did everything possible to modify his reading readiness lessons and make them interesting, but nothing seemed to work. The curriculum Mrs. Blaire was using offered little opportunity for children like Germain to use their creativity and imagination.

Try as I might, I was unable to find ways to modify the lessons such that Germain might learn the material through play and creative expression. By the end of the school year, I felt as though I'd done a great disservice to him. Much of my time with him had been spent evaluating and reevaluating his visual abilities and pre-reading skills. Presumably, I had been doing these evaluations to help him. Instead, my work with him seemed to have just the opposite effect. The happy child who had greeted me in September and who saw himself as one who "could," was now a child who saw himself as one who "couldn't" — couldn't see well, couldn't cut paper easily, couldn't read print, and couldn't recognize friends from across the room. I was frustrated. I had failed to help Germain see himself as one who "could" — who could carry on an interesting conversation, could figure out shape puzzles, could recognize things tactually, and could recognize his friends anywhere if they would just say, "Hi." Instead, I had offered Germain nothing but reminders of his handicap. As the end of the school year rolled around, I realized that I had been witness to — and an accomplice in — the diminishing of his self-confidence. Germain, who had started the year eager to learn, was now resisting all attempts to learn.

A summer of inspiration and reminiscence

When the academic year drew to a close, I felt relief. I needed the summer months to recoup and decided that I would spend time with my husband, David, and our then two-year-old son, Christian, and do some research on teaching strategies. Since I'd spent my last five summers attending school, I set a decidedly leisurely pace. First, I simply reconsidered my motivation to be a teacher.

One afternoon, while Christian napped, I took out a box of old class notes. As I sifted through the box, I unearthed long forgotten notes that I'd taken when I was attending the University of Pacific's Raymond College. Looking through the pages of those worn notes reminded me of the enthusiasm I once had for the teaching I was now doing.

With a glass of iced tea in hand, I stretched out on the living room couch and began to read the notes from my class on teaching math. The first page was headed, "Division by Repetitive Subtraction." As I slipped back to that time, I remembered the many different ways our professor had taught us algorithms for addition, subtraction, multiplication, and division. He'd shown us that math could be taught using Tangrams, balances, Base Ten Blocks, Fraction Bars, Geoboards, Cuisenaire Rods, Attribute Blocks and common board games. Using our fingers, we had learned to compute numbers that reached into the hundreds and thousands. Ten years before, I had sat on the floor of that classroom, learning to enjoy mathematical exploration, and beginning to understand that teaching offered marvelous opportunities for helping children make their own discoveries about the world. Now, I began to realize how far I'd strayed from those possibilities, and saw that my present work was not offering me the opportunity to be that innovative teacher I'd once dreamed of being.

Finishing the iced tea, I put aside my math notes and picked up a spiral notebook labeled "Educational Theory." Glued to the inside cover of the notebook was the class syllabus. Among other things, it listed titles of books that had been required reading. The first two were books by John Holt: *How Children Fail* and *How Children Learn.* I remembered that those books had been quite inspiring and decided that re-reading them would be a good place to begin my summer of reconsideration.

That afternoon, with Christian in tow, I headed for the library in search of books by Holt. I was surprised to find that he was such a prolific writer and I checked out *How Children Fail, How Children Learn, What Do I Do Monday?* and *Freedom and Beyond.*

That evening I began reading *How Children Fail.* The preface began: "Most children in school fail," and continued:

Why do they fail?

They fail because they are afraid, bored, and confused.

They are afraid, above all else, of failing, of disappointing or displeasing the many anxious adults around them, whose limitless hopes and expectations for them hang over their heads like a cloud.

They are bored because the things they are given and told to do in school are so trivial, so dull, and make such limited and narrow demands on the wide spectrum of their intelligence, capabilities, and talents.

They are confused because most of the torrent of words that pours over them in school makes little or no sense. It often flatly contradicts other things they have been told, and hardly ever has any relation to what they really know — to the rough model of reality that they carry around in their minds.

It was a jolt to read these words, and yet I knew they spoke the truth that I had experienced myself. Holt seemed to sum up my personal experience as a child in school, and now his words had a bearing on my experience as a teacher.

A few days later while I was reading *How Children Learn*, I was struck by Holt's discussion of an article entitled "Messing About In Science," by Professor David Hawkins, that had appeared in the February 1965 issue of *Science and Children*. In the article, Professor Hawkins talked about the necessity of allowing children to "mess about" with things before educators superimposed their instruction on the children. In this way, children can create a natural awareness of the things they are working with before they are asked to think about them in the abstract. Such "messing about" was completely unstructured and lasted for a few weeks. In summary, Holt had this to say:

This applies just as strongly to reading, or numbers, or arithmetic, or history, or geography, or language, as it does to science. Children need what we rarely give them in school — time for "Messing About" with reading — before they start trying to learn to read, to make the connections between letters and sounds. They need time to build up in their minds, without hurry, without pressure, a sense of what words look like, before they start trying to memorize particular words. In the same way, they need time for "Messing About" with numbers and numerals, before they start — if they ever should start — trying to memorize addition facts and multiplication tables. They need to know how big 76 is, or 134, or 35,000, or a million. They need to see, again without hurry or pressure, how numbers change and grow and relate to each other. They need to build up a mental model of the territory before they start trying to talk about it. We teachers like to think that we can transplant our own mental models into the minds of children by means of explanations. It can't be done.

I could hardly believe it! Thinking about my current dilemmas as a teacher, here was Holt saying that I should have given Germain all the play time he needed before superimposing "reading readiness" on his world. When I considered this, it seemed that the only fit thing for me to do was to try to facilitate Germain's learning accordingly.

Germain enters kindergarten

As I continued to read more of John Holt's words, I developed a gnawing sense that Germain's problems may have just begun. Determined to prevent further teaching failures, I took time before school started to educate the school staff who would have Germain as a student. I took particular care to spend lots of time with Ms. Fredericks, his kindergarten teacher.

Ms. Fredericks was very friendly, seemed full of enthusiasm, and had many questions for me. Her classroom seemed particularly well-suited to Germain's needs. Besides having ample natural lighting, the presence of small learning centers indicated that individually-paced learning was provided for. As we talked, it was clear that Ms. Fredericks was well-organized, willing to suggest lesson adaptations, and willing to incorporate the adaptive suggestions I made. At the end of our first meeting, I was feeling as though Germain would have a better experience than he had had the previous year.

On Monday of the following week, Germain began attending afternoon kindergarten. Since he was new to the school, I met with him there on his first day. He was excited to be in school and seemed glad to see me. We spent our first afternoon together in Ms. Frederick's room, getting acquainted with the other children and learning about classroom expectations. At the end of the day, I walked Germain to the bus and told him I would see him on Wednesday. He was happy.

During Germain's first weeks at school, I taught him the layout of the building and reviewed the braille alphabet with him. Although the school's hallways were poorly lit, Germain loved learning his way about. During these walks, he met most of the staff and, on subsequent walks, when he met the same people, he remembered their names.

"You're Mrs. Beedle, aren't you?," he'd say with excitement. Mrs. Beedle would smile broadly and ask, "How did you remember my name?"

"I'm just good with names, that's all."

Germain was proud of his ability to remember the names of his school's janitor, librarian, cook, principal, secretary, and the various teachers he came across. This made our orientation sessions particularly rewarding.

Braille review sessions also offered Germain a chance to demonstrate his abilities. "I can remember how to write my name; do you want to see how I can do it?" I was delighted that he wanted to show me what he remembered, and I watched intently. As he wrote he said, "First there is the 'dot six' for the capital sign," and he pressed the correct key with his pinkie finger. After writing the "G," he explained: "My name has the 'er' contraction next," and carefully placed five fingers on the correct keys and simultaneously pressed down hard to make the embossed sign for "er." After feeling to see if his embossing was clear so far, he said, "The next two letters are just letters," and wrote "m" and "a." "Now comes the 'in' contraction." He simultaneously pressed down hard on the "dot three," "dot five" keys. It had been two months since he had written his name or seen it written, and he remembered it perfectly. He was proud of himself and I told him how impressed I was with his work. This first review session went smoothly, as did subsequent ones.

After a month of school, Ms. Fredericks began teaching the children about the alphabet and consonant sounds. Germain was well-prepared for the work and he seemed to be excited about using his braille writer in class. In fact, it seemed as though he'd matured some and was really eager to get on with learning to read. Like every other student, Ms. Fredericks assigned Germain a work space at one of the five tables in the room. There he kept his brailler and paper just as the other children kept their pencils and paper.

Germain has his first setbacks

Germain was happy at first. With a little effort, he could keep up with the instruction. The lessons were simple: practice writing particular letters.

After the first few weeks, however, Ms. Fredericks began giving the children more complex worksheets. These worksheets required learning skills such as matching uppercase letters in one column with lowercase letters in a second column. As I brailled the lessons for Germain, I could foresee the difficulties he might come up against. With Ms. Fredericks' consent, I introduced the work to Germain before it was presented to the class. My lessons gave him a chance to learn to use his fingers as markers, between which he could draw the beginning and the end of the line that would be used to connect the uppercase "A" in one column with the lowercase "a" in the next column. Germain caught on easily. But one afternoon, as our time was ending, Germain said, "This is getting too hard." I didn't understand and asked him what he meant.

"Ms. Fredericks won't show me the work sheet until we sit at our tables." As we put his crayons and paper away and rushed to get ready for the bus, I made a mental note to speak with Ms. Fredericks.

The next day, I brought this up. "Germain said that the worksheets are getting too difficult for him. Is he having difficulty in class?"

She said, "There's no real problem that I can think of. When I am explaining the worksheets, I expect the children to sit quietly and listen to my instruction. Then I dismiss them and they go to their desks to do the work."

I asked, "I don't understand Germain's statement, though. Do the other children get their worksheets before he gets his?"

"No, they are to look at me and pay attention to the sample worksheet I use to demonstrate the lesson."

Now I understood. Germain couldn't see what Ms. Fredericks was holding up for the other children to see. He was being asked to listen and understand spoken directions while the other children could listen and see the worksheets Ms. Fredericks was holding up. This problem should be easy to rectify.

As a vision teacher, a significant part of my job was to educate teachers about the real world of blind children. Such children did not have, as some teachers believed, a superior sense of hearing enabling them to listen and understand what was being written on a blackboard. Germain could not understand his worksheet without having a chance to see it. I was confident that Ms. Fredericks would understand the limitations of a blind child's ability to form visualizations from spoken words. "Ms. Fredericks, I think Germain is having difficulty doing the work because he can't create a visual image of your worksheet as you or I can. He needs to see, with his hands, in order to understand." I paused, waiting for her to respond in some way. She didn't, so I continued, "When you are giving classroom demonstrations, could you let Germain see with his hands what the other children are seeing with their eyes?"

Much to my surprise, Ms. Fredericks couldn't understand Germain's situation. Her response was, "No, I can't do that. If I give him his sheet before all the other children get theirs, they will all want the same treatment." She paused and thought about what she had said and then continued, "No. Giving out the worksheets to all the children ahead of time will cause too much distraction. The children won't listen well to my directions." This response was dismaying, to say the least.

I could see that it was going to be hard to persuade Ms. Fredericks to change her mind. She had her hands full with twenty active kindergartners and needed to minimize distractions. My task was to try to persuade her to see things from Germain's point of view. Over the course of the next few weeks, I tried to advocate gently for adapting the classroom procedure to help Germain. But no words of persuasion seemed to help. Day after day, Germain sat and listened to directions without a worksheet on his lap to look at. I began to notice that his work was suffering, and yet all I could do was encourage him to listen carefully. I promised him that I was doing my best to get things changed, and he cheerfully agreed to keep up his good work.

Creative adaptations by a creative child

In the weeks that followed, Germain did the best he could. One afternoon I happened to be in the classroom as Ms. Fredericks was giving directions for the daily worksheets. Out of curiosity, I kept an eye on Germain to see how he managed. When the children were dismissed from the circle and went to their desks, Germain went into action. He immediately began chatting with the two children sitting on either side of him. Soon I noticed that they were offering him their worksheets to look at. Germain's vision was very limited, but by picking up papers and holding them close to his face he could follow along as the children gave him directions. After figuring out the sheet, he worked independently with the braille copy of his worksheet. I was amazed that he'd worked out such a simple solution to his problem, and when we worked together that afternoon I told him so. I said he seemed to have found a better solution to his problem than either of his two teachers had!

A week or two later, Ms. Fredericks complained to me that Germain was being disruptive. Although she saw the value in the system he had worked out, she felt it interrupted the other children too much. I was dismayed and a bit confused, but I agreed to talk to Germain and see what could be done.

My heart wasn't in it. Telling Germain that he wouldn't be allowed to ask his friends for help seemed all wrong to me. Indeed, I had suggested to some of my other students that they do just the same: check with their classmates when they were unsure of assignments. In most instances, other teachers had been happy that my students had reliable friends to help them. Such help saved time for the teacher and provided appropriate opportunities for socialization among the children. I tried to think of a positive way to break the news to Germain that he shouldn't talk to his tablemates about the daily work. Finally I hit upon an idea. "Germain, Ms. Fredericks really wants to be the only one to help you with your worksheets. Can you be sure to ask her when you need help instead of asking Billy, Juan, Aisha or Pam?"

After taking in this idea for a few moments, Germain said, "OK."

As I had suggested, Germain began asking Ms. Fredericks for help. One afternoon, I observed Germain and Ms. Fredericks working together. She was helping him cut out shapes from one page and place them on a second page to form a train engine. He held the drawing close to his eyes to see the black lines and feel the embossing I'd done as he listened intently to Ms. Fredericks' directions. I was encouraged and relieved that, finally, there seemed to be an appropriate way for Germain to get the instruction he needed.

But as the school term drew to a close, I could sense that Ms. Fredericks was becoming irritated with Germain. When I asked her how things were going, she said she was frustrated because of the inordinate amount of time she spent explaining lessons to Germain. This was taking time from her other students. It was apparent that her frustrations had been building for quite some time. She talked to me about many things: not only about the individualized instruction, but that Germain wasn't trying hard enough, he wasn't listening to group directions, it took him too long to do his work, his work wasn't very neat, and that his behavior was deteriorating. As she recited this litany, it was clear that she felt Germain didn't deserve the individual help that she gave him.

I could easily understand her frustrations, yet I knew that Germain was trying to do the best he could. Germain's questions were not being attended to when he sat, without a worksheet, trying to listen to instructions. Not allowed to ask his classmates for help, he had to rely on his teacher for assistance, and since she was frustrated with this situation, she was less willing to give him individual attention. He was losing interest in his work. It had become a vicious circle. I could see that if Ms. Fredericks and I couldn't come up with a solution to this problem, Germain might lose patience with school work altogether. I wanted to avoid this at all costs.

As diplomatically as I could, I tried to make Ms. Fredericks understand that Germain's behavior was directly linked to the frustrations he was experiencing. Unfortunately, she didn't see things this way. She felt that he needed "to adapt to the situation" and learn to work just like the rest of her class seemed to be doing. As I pursued my line of reasoning, she became defensive and less tolerant of anything I suggested.

Poor Germain! As winter set in, a familiar pattern emerged. More and more, Germain was being sent to sit in the hall for misbehaving. He stopped paying attention to his lessons. As in his preschool days, he worked well when he was interested in the subject matter and became resistant when the lessons didn't meet his needs. When Germain and I worked on reading and writing, or lessons his teacher had offered to the class but that he had been unable to do on his own, Germain was an eager worker. He was eager because I allowed him to work in ways in which he experienced success. I let him hold worksheets close to his good eye while I explained directions to him. I gave him extra time to finish complicated lessons. I allowed for paper-shape cutting that was not perfect because Germain was proud to have been able to cut along the line at all. I allowed for drawings that did not meet my visual expectations because they met *his* visual expectations. In all these situations, Germain demonstrated a willingness to listen and learn.

Unfortunately, during the remainder of Germain's school day he was being victimized by a system that was designed to deal with children who have no individualized needs or interests. Ms. Fredericks was failing him because she was unable to see the complexity of the situation. Instead, she gradually came to see Germain's difficulties as caused by something inherent in him. She had displaced her failings as a teacher on Germain's shoulders and labeled him a "behavior problem" rather than considering her own and the system's unfortunate contributions. Both of these failures had unhappy consequences.

Things fall apart

In Ms. Fredericks' classroom, Germain's behavior continued to deteriorate. Soon his frustrations with Ms. Fredericks were spilling over into our work sessions. As his behavior began to disrupt gym, art and library times, Ms. Fredericks recommended that Germain be tested for placement in a program for children with learning disabilities and behavior problems. Unfortunately, this set into motion a long chain of events that eventually defeated Germain.

First, there was the testing that he went through. His examiners determined that he had no learning disability and in fact was far too bright for the program. Ms. Fredericks asked that Germain be considered for the program on the basis of his behavior alone. Although I understood her desire to have Germain removed from her class, I couldn't help but remember my summer reading. Holt's books had reminded me that learning shouldn't be stressful. Rather it should be enjoyable. According to what I'd read, it seemed clear that the school environment was at the root of Germain's problems.

Secondly, his evaluation was reconsidered. During this period of reconsideration, his family moved and Germain began attending a new school. He experienced success in his new school but the evaluation team concluded that Germain could benefit from placement in the program for children with behavior problems. Unfortunately, Germain's new teacher and the school social worker were unwilling, despite my arguments, to ask that Germain remain in his new school. They felt that if his previous teacher saw a need for special programming, it would be in his best interests to go along with those recommendations. No words of persuasion, even from his mother, could convince the staff that such a placement was unnecessary. By June, we received word that Germain had been recommended for placement in the self-contained SLBP (Slow Learning, Behavior Problem) program located across town.

Another summer passes

Once again, I began my summer feeling as though I was completely failing Germain. With another summer on my hands and no classes to attend, I set out to put all thoughts of failure behind me and enjoy myself. At that time David and I lived in Minneapolis across the street from a major corporation's headquarters. That spring, it had begun to remodel and expand its facility, and our son, Christian, being a typically curious three-year-old, became interested in the goings-on. As summer got underway, he became fascinated by the work that was being done. During the course of that summer and the following year, that building project shook not only the foundations of our house but also my understanding of how easily children teach themselves.

The noises, shaking windows, and clouds of dust that the earthmovers, cranes and bulldozers brought to our neighborhood captivated Christian. Whenever he could, he would climb up on the couch by our living room window and stand there for hours watching all the activity. It amazed me that he found so much enjoyment in simply watching construction workers pour concrete, lay bricks, hoist steel beams with a huge crane, or direct traffic around the delivery trucks that frequently blocked our street. Watching this activity became an everyday routine for him.

Christian's observations soon became the focal point of his learning. His interest in watching the crane operators, dump truck drivers, traffic controllers and builders soon expanded. On our weekly trip to the library, we hunted for books about trucks and construction crews. Christian had me help him find books on trucks and then asked me to read from them. If he liked the stories I read, he would select those books to take home for the week. Once he got the books home, he'd have us read them to him repeatedly. When we weren't reading to him, he would spend hours and hours on his own studying the pictures in the library books. Sometimes he'd be quiet for so long that my "mothering alarm" would ring. Was he doing something he shouldn't? Had he hurt himself? I'd go to his room and there he'd be, buried in a pile of books. If I listened carefully, I could hear him whispering to himself about this or that character, or about Mike Mulligan's steam shovel. He was absorbed in his own important world and he obviously loved it there.

When he wasn't watching the construction project or reading books about earthmovers, Christian created his own world of construction projects using his blocks, Legos and toy trucks. His blocks became the cities and streets built by him and his imaginary construction crews. He used Legos to construct buildings and other vehicles. Then I noticed a wonderful thing was happening: as Christian observed the construction crew and played with his own books, trucks and blocks, he began to learn the basic skills of counting, color identification and reading!

Christian's keen interest in the construction project and his self-made building projects lasted beyond the summer months. It was something he enjoyed and came back to day after day. He was consumed with the joy of playing-and-learning, and his joy reminded me that learning can be an exhilarating experience. As I thought about his happiness and the natural ease of his learning, I began to realize that his learning experience was ideal. He was enthusiastic, self-directed, unstructured, comfortable, and productive.

At home there was no curriculum guiding Christian's learning. He simply learned whatever and however he wanted. With such freedom, Christian's learning surpassed anything I had been trained to believe was possible. As I recognized this, and was reminded of how I'd learned about the world of blind students at my mother's side, I knew that I only half-heartedly believed that Germain needed to sit still and complete the lessons I gave him.

When I had first met Germain, I was quick to notice his curiosity, spunk, and facility with language. In fact, I had rarely seen such a vivacious child in all my work in elementary, middle, and high schools. At that time, Germain displayed all of the characteristics I was now noticing in my own son: an interest in learning about *his* world, fascination with games which centered around *his* interests; in other words, he was self- motivated. Like millions of other children before him, Germain had learned, without the assistance of teachers and lesson plans, to talk, walk and use his imagination as a tool to guide his learning. From my current perspective, it seemed that the only thing I'd done for Germain was to put him on a collision course with failure.

Christian and Germain spent most of their preschool years playing. Both children seemed to learn best when they were immersed in their play. The difference arose when my *job* required that I take Germain away from *his* world of play and force both of us into the artificial roles of "teacher" and "student." With Christian, I was a "teacher" only in the sense that I facilitated the learning that he sought by himself. The similarities between the learning needs of these two children, and the contrast between the roles I played when I was with each child, made me realize that the best teaching environment didn't look like a school at all. It was, instead, an environment defined and energized solely by the child's need to learn. Where was such a school?

A new alternative: homeschooling

As I pondered this question, a friend of mine was looking for the "perfect" kindergarten for her son, Clayton. Jean was visiting schools in hopes of finding one that would complement Clayton's preschool Montessori experience.

Since I would be going through the same process soon, I stood to learn something from her experience. We often found ourselves in conversation about her discoveries. One afternoon, Jean mentioned that she had read about something called "homeschooling." My ears perked up. She said she had read an interesting interview about homeschooling in the July/August 1980 issue of *Mother Earth News*. Since we subscribed to that magazine, that evening I rummaged through our pile of back issues until I found the one I was looking for. As I skimmed the table of contents looking for the interview, my eyes were immediately drawn to the words "John Holt." He was the person being interviewed!

Eagerly I started to read. Within minutes, I felt the excitement I had felt the summer before when I re-discovered his books. In that interview,

Holt's words echoed my own experiences:

"It's a well established principle that if you take somebody who's doing something for her or his own pleasure and offer some kind of outside reward for doing it — and let the person become accustomed to performing the task for the reward — then take the reward away, the individual will stop that activity. You can even train nursery school youngsters who love to draw pictures to stop drawing them, simply by giving them gold stars or some other little bonus for a couple of months...and then removing the artificial motivation."

This was Holt's personal experience. As a preschool child, he had taught himself to read. By the time he entered school, he was already infused with a love of language, reading and music. But twelve years later, when he graduated from high school, he wouldn't read unless it was an assigned task. After years and years in school, he had lost his interest in reading because the motivation to read had been taken from him.

Instantly, I saw my teaching experiences flash before me: there was Corrine, a self-taught reader who wasn't allowed to move two grade levels ahead so that the reading required of her would be interesting and challenging; and Amy, who didn't understand why she must learn "greater than" and "less than"; and Raoul, who didn't have any interest in writing a report on wolves; and Peter, who enjoyed music so much that it was all that he did when he had free time; and Germain, who didn't fit into the system of schooling as it was being offered to him. All of these children were being robbed of the chance to truly enjoy learning. It was clear that I owed it to myself, to our son and to all of my students to investigate this homeschooling alternative.

☙ Chapter 2 ❧

Observations In The Schoolhouse

...This was a teacher "so obsessed with the right answer hidden in her mind, that she could not think about what [the student] was really saying and thinking, could not see that his reasoning was logical and correct."
— *John Holt,* How Children Fail

AS AN ENTHUSIASTIC STUDENT TEACHER, I sat observing my master teacher introduce her first grade students to the mathematical symbols for "greater than" and "less than" (">" and "<"). She had a talent for using creative stories to get her lessons across and I marveled at this ability. To explain these symbols, she told the children:

"Just remember Big Al the Alligator. Big Al only likes eating BIG numbers. Whenever Big Al has a choice between eating a bigger number or a smaller number, he'll always choose the bigger number. As Big Al gets ready to eat the big number, he opens his mouth very wide, just like this."

With her chalk she wrote on the board: 3>2   5<9   4>1   3<10

"See, this is how simple it is."

When the children were dismissed to do their work, I circulated among them.

Soon a little girl came up to me and showed me her book. She was crying. "*Why?*" she asked, "*I don't understand this.*" I tried reminding her about Big Al but this didn't seem to help her in the least. Still crying, she asked, "*Why do we have to use this? What does it mean? Why do we have to do this?*"

I empathized with the little girl's feelings of distress and confusion, but I didn't know how to answer her. How many times had I, as a child, experienced similar frustrations and never had them resolved? Although many of my teachers were able to show me *how* to get the right answer, they failed me when I wanted to understand *why* it was important. For instance, long division had seemed a waste of time to me and I couldn't understand when I would ever need it. I had been unable to grasp the logical relationships between dividing small and large numbers: when we were told that dividing 6000 by 300 was just like dividing 6 by 3, I couldn't understand the explanation.

Observing this little girl's frustration and remembering my own reminded me of why I had wanted to teach: I didn't want children to learn hollow lessons without understanding. I didn't want to become the type of teacher John Holt had described in *How Children Fail*: one who was "so obsessed with the right answer hidden in her mind, that she could not think about what he (the student) was really saying and thinking, could not see that his reasoning was logical and correct." I wanted my lessons to be guided by the child's understanding rather than some arbitrary notion of what children "needed" to learn.

The self-directed learner

I'd spent my entire summer reading all of the back issues of John Holt's newsletter, *Growing Without Schooling*. The reading was quite informative, giving me an understanding of the self-directed learning process that homeschooling could offer. I began to compare what I had read about self-directed learning to what I knew about how children learn in school.

According to Holt, self-directed learning emerges from childhood play. As a teacher, I had already developed an intuitive understanding of this concept. In my earliest interactions with Germain, I had used play as the basis of my lessons. Through simple games, Germain had learned to look for colors, identify shapes and understand spatial relationships. Likewise, his braille readiness, listening skills and travel techniques had been acquired by using games.

I didn't need to look very far to understand that play was more than just a useful teaching tool. It was, as Holt said, the basis of childhood learning. In my daily comings and goings, I was surrounded by children who learned from their play — about gardening, history, auto mechanics, art, and much more.

For example, when I worked in our cooperative vegetable garden, I worked alongside a four-year-old who loved to imagine he was a farmer. When the adults were busy weeding and harvesting, Drew helped. And, from pretending to be a farmer, he progressed to *becoming* a farmer. His ability to tell the difference between a weed and newly-sprouting carrots or beets soon outshone mine! When in doubt about what to pull, I usually turned to Farmer Drew for assistance.

In another instance, Ian, a friend of Christian's, became a novice historian through play. When Ian came to play, it was common for the boys to play wildly imaginative games, often involving monsters and superheroes. One afternoon, Ian covered our three living room chairs with blankets, creating a "land of volcanos." When Christian asked what the volcanos were for, Ian said, "I want to play Tyrannosaurus Rex." The words "Tyrannosaurus Rex" were new to Christian, so he asked Ian what they meant. Ian told him, "Tyrannosaurus Rex was a huge monster who lived on earth before people came." As Christian asked more questions, Ian gave him an introductory lesson on the prehistoric era. Soon Ian was "teaching" Christian about the many types of dinosaurs that once roamed the earth, their habitat and the types of food that different dinosaurs ate. As Ian talked, he climbed onto one of the chairs over which he'd draped a blanket and threw the blanket to the floor, making great rumbling noises as he did so. When he'd finished playing the role of an erupting volcano, he jumped to the floor and enacted the part of Tyrannosaurus Rex dying in the fires set off by the volcano. The entire time he was engaged in this game, he was telling Christian why dinosaurs no longer roamed the earth. For the rest of the afternoon, our living room was alive with erupting volcanos and dying dinosaurs — and lessons in paleontology.

The end of the prehistoric era, as enacted in our living room, gave way to other games, like "auto mechanic." In those days, we owned a bright yellow Honda Civic. My days on the road as an itinerant teacher had put many thousands of miles on it, and toward the end of its life, David spent many hours under its hood trying to coax a few more miles out of its weary engine. Christian enjoyed watching his dad tinker and was soon learning the names of tools and engine parts. One afternoon, Christian put this knowledge to use in his own imaginative way.

Ian and Christian had spent much of the afternoon racing their big wheels up and down the block. When this got boring, Christian suggested that they fix their "cars." Within minutes, Christian was showing Ian imaginary spark plugs, fan belts, oil filters, master cylinders and gaskets. With imaginary socket wrenches, dwell meters and timing lights, Christian and Ian spent the rest of the afternoon tuning their "race cars" and giving them test drives.

On another afternoon, when the weather was particularly bad, Christian had his friend Becca over, and painting was the focal point of their play. I covered the dining room floor with old newspapers and gave the children large sheets of blank newsprint to work on. Within minutes they had discovered that they could mix their supply of primary colors into a vast rainbow. By afternoon's end, each child had made over twenty different colors and had used them in as many paintings.

In each of these situations, and many more besides, these children were engrossed in play while simultaneously learning. These observations made it easy for me to understand that Holt was onto something: children love to learn.

Older children love learning too!

Of course, discovering that young children love to learn was not that remarkable. But Holt and many parents testified that love of learning through play does not necessarily die out as children get older. As children get older, we simply call play that becomes learning by different names, most commonly "self-directed learning."

The parents who wrote the stories for *Growing Without Schooling* helped me understand this. As a teacher, I'd been trained to believe that self-directed learning could only emerge *after* mandatory instruction had been absorbed. Never had it crossed my mind that, given freedom to learn, all children, even those who are beyond age three, four or five, are natural self-directed learners. Reading through the pages of *Growing Without Schooling* made it clear that all children are capable of teaching themselves — with the guidance and support of parents, mentors and peers — the most complex of tasks, including (but not limited to) reading, writing and math.

These descriptions showed children learning all manner of things at home and in their communities. With the ease that comes with doing things naturally, they were learning complex skills of reading, writing, arithmetic, business management, vocal and instrumental music, horsemanship, radio engineering, astronomy, animal breeding, and more. What was important, though, was that these children were not being "instructed" according to a curriculum written by adults. Instead, they were given the freedom to explore these interests by "playing at them" and then participating in real-world experiences as their confidence and abilities grew.

For example, children who played "store" were able to follow their imaginations into real life experiences. If their interest in games of "store" were deep-seated, their parents helped them find ways to volunteer in real stores. For some, these volunteer opportunities became paying jobs when they got older. Other children turned gazing at the stars into self-motivated quests to learn about the constellations and telescopes. As their interests grew, reading skills emerged and mentors were sought. Some of these amateur astronomers I read about sought membership in astronomy clubs, and this provided them opportunities to meet real astronomers who could help them with their studies of the universe.

Just as the children who had turned their fantasy of working in a store or being an astronomer into real life experiences, so too did children who were interested in radio work and television. With encouragement and support from their parents, these children were finding opportunities to do pre-production work on radio and television shows, to engineer those shows, and even write and produce their own shows.

As all of these children — the retail volunteer, the budding astronomer, the radio and television aficionado — immersed themselves in "play," they took on "adult" responsibilities which, in turn, brought them into contact with more opportunities to learn.

Reading about these older children developing youthful fantasies into true interests in the adult world, I began to understand what I had been missing in my teaching. The children described in the pages of *Growing Without Schooling* were the children I had imagined myself working with, children who, for the most part, directed their own learning and simply needed a guiding hand from time to time.

My childhood fantasy of having my students work at their own pace in ways which nurtured their learning seemed to have come true in this world of homeschooling. These homeschooled children were learning everything imaginable. Interested learners greedily acquired reading skills, although they didn't all necessarily begin to read at age five. Some might not need that skill until they were ten or twelve, but eventually, their strong interests in various subjects made reading a necessity and they learned to read, driven by their interest. Similarly, children might not learn math skills until they worked with a carpenter, or a computer programmer, or in retail sales. In these situations, children selected the time, the pace and the subject matter. Rather than having adults foisting lessons on them, they were free to choose who their teachers would be, what the lessons were, and when those lessons would be given. As Holt had said, self-directed learners are quite capable of getting the education they need. For them, administration, curriculum and teachers were unnecessary. Each person a child sought out for instruction was both an administrator and a teacher who provided the "curriculum."

By the time I completed my summer reading, I was well on my way to being a confirmed believer in self-directed learning for children. The more I read about children who were allowed to learn at their own pace, the more I became convinced that enthusiasm for learning could be maintained throughout a lifetime.

I make an informal survey of children in school

Now it was time to resume my work as a teacher. When I returned to work, I set out to do some careful observation; I wanted to see whether or not such enthusiasm persisted in the lives of schooled children.

Unlike most teachers, my work with visually-impaired students took me into a variety of schools: rural, suburban, inner city; private, parochial, and public. I worked with children of all ages: preschoolers, elementary schoolers, middle schoolers, high schoolers, and an occasional adult. These different experiences offered me a unique opportunity to observe the faces and moods of children who were being taught according to traditional teaching methods. I began paying attention to all that I was seeing.

As I had expected, children in the early years seemed to be happy with school. Most of the children I observed enjoyed all that school offered: learning new skills, field trips, special visitors, holiday art projects, lunch in the cafeteria, recess and special assemblies. Most of them displayed a cheerful and enthusiastic attitude.

By third or fourth grade, I noticed that students displayed a marked change in attitude. The novelty of days punctuated by learning new skills, field trips, special assemblies, recess, and new friendships, seemed to have worn off. Although most students were compliant and did the work their teachers asked them to do, the cheerful and enthusiastic attitude they once possessed seemed to have faded. Generally speaking, these were the years that the first whisperings of dissatisfaction and boredom with school surfaced.

The middle school years seemed to mark yet another change. With puberty, students seemed to be more interested in socializing than in what their teachers were trying to impart. Although most children I had contact with were good students, "getting by" seemed to be the order of the day. Unless rewards were promised (extra credit, being excused from an assignment, special privileges, etc.), most of them weren't interested in pursuing their academic studies beyond the required minimum.

As I observed students in high school, they seemed to fall into five groups: highly motivated, college-bound students; college-bound kids who were not very motivated; students who were planning to go to technical schools or other work training programs; students who were going to go directly into the work force; and students who were ready to drop out at any minute. Highly motivated college-bound students genuinely liked doing their school work, and were involved with student government, athletic teams and school clubs. They enjoyed the school atmosphere and the opportunities it offered. Less-motivated college-bound students were capable of academic success but seemed to be unsure of any particular direction in life. Although they believed that without a college education their life prospects would be limited, they seemed unable to think clearly about career possibilities.

For those students heading toward technical school or a job, some seemed ready to move on, while others didn't know what else to do with themselves. It was rare for any of these students to be involved in student government or academically-focused school clubs, and participation in athletic programs was limited because their grade point averages weren't high enough. My feeling about many of these students was that they might, in fact, be some of the most creative students in the school, but, unfortunately, most school settings did not nurture their creativity.

Students who were close to dropping out clearly displayed a negative attitude. I couldn't help but wonder how many of them were like Germain — creative but totally frustrated in a school where their learning needs were not met. Might not these students have been "success stories" had they been offered opportunities to be self-directed learners?

From observing children in school, I now had more questions than answers. I'd gone searching for the bright-eyed, eager children I'd seen on school district promotional packages, curriculum advertisements and in education textbooks, but had found few. Were the only students who really flourished in school those who were "gifted" or could easily adapt to traditional teaching methods?

Show-and-tell: it could be better

My work offered me many opportunities to observe classroom routines. Sometimes I helped individual students at the back of classrooms; on other occasions I team-taught lessons with teachers who had my student in their classes.

One morning, I chanced to sit in on a kindergarten "show and tell." As I pulled up a miniature chair and settled in at the back of Ms. Murdock's class, my attention was drawn to a young boy sitting on the floor in front of me, bursting at the seams with eagerness. Three children were called on to share their stories before Joseph was given the honor. He beamed as he came forward to stand beside Ms. Murdock's chair. He had two fistfuls of brightly colored pipe cleaners.

Ms. Murdock asked, "What do you have, Joseph?"

"My name spelled in pipe cleaners!"

"When did you make this, Joseph?"

"Last night. Mom brought home new pipe cleaners. She let me make this last night and this morning before school."

It was quite clear that Joseph had spent quite a bit of time bending his pipe cleaners so that they would resemble each letter in his name.

"Ms. Murdock, can you help me hold it up so everyone can see?"

There was a slight pause as Joseph sorted through his multi-colored assortment of shapes and began handing them to his teacher. Her first comment caught me off guard: "Joseph, what's this? This doesn't look like a 'J,' does it class?"

The children dutifully responded, "No," as Joseph continued sorting out his letters. He was so involved in his work that he really didn't hear these initial comments.

As more letters were untangled from Joseph's collection and handed to Ms. Murdock, she continued to slight his work. "Your 'S' is larger than your 'J'." It was true that the letters weren't all even in size or perfect in shape, but the work did display thought and diligent effort. As the moments passed, Joseph began to take in what was being said. His once-bright face began to show a look of concern. Ms. Murdock dismissed him with the words, "Boys and girls, let's thank Joseph," which was followed by a chorus of "Thank yous." As he headed back to his seat on the floor, the words, "Next time, Joseph, make it so we can all read it," came as a final blow. Clearly he felt shamed for his efforts. During the remaining ten minutes of show-and-tell, he never seemed to regain his smile.

I observed a similar situation in a small suburban school. At the appointed time, I arrived in the kindergarten room to meet with my student, Kathy, and I sat with her on the floor, as the show-and-tell session got underway. One by one, the teacher, Mrs. Simon, began calling on those who were ready to share their treasures. As a child finished his or her presentation, those in the audience would beg, "Me! Me! Let me have a turn!," accompanying their pleas with vigorous arm waving. Using facial expressions to express her displeasure with such behavior, Mrs. Simon was able to control the vocal outbursts. If she donned a stern expression, the children became very quiet — but at the same time kept waving their hands. During one of the "Me! Me!" intervals, Kathy, my student, raised her hand. When Mrs. Simon gave the children a menacing grimace, the group hushed itself, but Kathy, who could not see that the other children continued to wave their hands, quickly put her hand in her lap. Another child was called upon.

Seeing that Kathy was responding only to the auditory cues that she was receiving, I knew I had to intervene. I leaned forward and whispered in her ear, "Next time Mrs. Simon asks who else might like a turn, keep your hand up until she actually calls on someone." There was no time to explain that the other children kept their hands in the air. Mrs. Simon asked for more volunteers. Kathy's hand shot up and finally, she was given a turn.

"Yes, Kathy, what is it that you'd like to share?"

In hushed tones Kathy said, "I can button and unbutton." It was difficult to hear what she had said because she had a quiet voice and some of the children who were sitting around her were talking among themselves.

Instead of asking the children who were causing the disturbance to quiet down, Mrs. Simon belted out, "What?" This startled Kathy. Not only had the teacher's voice been unnecessarily loud, but it also expressed irritation. Kathy seemed to be confused by the response.

Kathy's face carried an expression of worry and apprehension. Again she spoke, though louder this time: "I can button and unbutton." It was apparent that she went unheard this time, too.

"WHAT?" Mrs. Simon said loudly, with the same irritated tone. Kathy was reluctant to go on, so I gave her an encouraging pat on the shoulder. Kathy had no idea that the talkative children were the source of Mrs. Simon's irritation.

As Mrs. Simon stood up and moved closer to Kathy, she maintained a facial expression that spoke quite clearly to the children seated on the floor, "Be quiet, or else," but not everyone, including Kathy, got the cue. Again Mrs. Simon boomed, "WHAT?"

With a bit of fear in her voice, Kathy answered, "I can button and unbutton!"

Mrs. Simon asked, "What can you button and unbutton?"

"My shirt," Kathy said.

With her irritation at the other children still present in her voice, Mrs. Simon responded, "Oh," and returned to her seat.

The look I saw on Kathy's face dismayed me. Moments before, she had been excited to share her achievements. Now she appeared to be on the verge of tears. Her trust that those around her would share in her joy seemed to have been shattered. I couldn't help but wonder how this experience would affect her eagerness to participate in future show-and-tell sessions.

These may seem like small, unimportant incidents, but I witnessed them over and over again. Had I not been attuned, by my reading in *Growing Without Schooling* to the subtle ways in which experiences like Kathy's and Joseph's had caused parents to start homeschooling their children, I might never have noticed that anything had gone awry. Now such behavior by teachers took on an entirely new meaning. I could no longer accept that such mistreatment of children, no matter how slight, was acceptable.

One morning while working in an inner city school, I witnessed another such instance. Josh was a first grade student with whom I worked. He was a beginning braille reader, so I spent a great deal of time with him in his classroom during reading period. Josh's teacher, Mr. Livingston, was a good teacher. He knew his craft and quite regularly came up with very creative lesson plans. On this particular morning, I found a seat and waited to work with Josh until Mr. Livingston had gone over the previous day's assignment and had explained the morning's worksheets.

On the previous day, the children had been working on initial consonant sounds and their homework was to make scrapbooks, each page of which was to be filled with pictures cut from magazines that illustrated a particular sound of either a consonant or consonant blend.

Mr. Livingston asked students to come forward with their homework sheets and share their answers with the class. The assignment had been to paste pictures of objects whose initial consonant sound was "S" onto a page titled "Words Beginning With S". First came John, who waved his hand so enthusiastically that Mr. Livingston called on him by saying, "John, I'm afraid that if I don't call on you right now you might fall out of your seat!" Everyone laughed, including me.

John almost ran to the front of the room to stand by Mr. Livingston.

He blurted out, "I found these pictures. They are 'sox,' 'shoes,' and 'sail-boat'."

I watched in astonishment as I saw Mr. Livingston tear the picture of the "shoes" off John's page. As he did so, he said, "I think we have to remove this picture, John." John looked on in disbelief as his work was being dismantled. "This is not the 's' sound but the 'sh' sound." When the picture of the shoes had been removed from the page, John's paper was returned to him and he returned to his seat. No mention was made of the good job John had done on the rest of his work.

Mr. Livingston called on a few more students and, to my dismay, he repeated the same process. Within minutes, the children became restless and agitated. Like me, they were having a hard time watching the pages being torn apart. Soon Mr. Livingston began calling groups of children to his table so that he could make corrections more efficiently. By the time each child's paper had been corrected, it was quite clear that few of them felt good about their first attempt at doing homework. I felt miserable for the children.

In the not-so-distant past, I might have been upset by what I had just witnessed, but I would not have thought that what Mr. Livingston had done was wrong. After all, the children needed to learn correct letter sounds, didn't they? On this day, though, I understood, from a place deep in my heart, that such treatment of children was wrong. The unthinking attitude with which Mr. Livingston treated the children's work showed no respect for their efforts. Although I understood that even under the best of circumstances, teachers couldn't always give their students individualized attention, I knew there must be better alternatives to what I had witnessed.

Learning by the bell

One of my main tasks as a vision teacher was to teach students skills that would enhance their independence within the classroom and, ultimately, in society. I was often frustrated by school bells that interrupted some of my most successful teaching moments. One of these occurred when I was teaching one of my students, Anna, to use an Optacon (a machine, no longer considered state-of-the-art, that allowed braille readers tactual access to the printed page).

Soon after beginning to teach Anna how to use her Optacon, I began to feel frustrated with our lessons. The school bells signaling the end of the hour interrupted us at the most inopportune times. At the end of three weeks (six 48-minute time blocks), Anna voiced her own frustrations. "Why can't I just stay here for the rest of the day and learn how to use this machine? That's all it would really take, anyway." She was obviously eager to become an independent reader and the bell cutting our lessons short was interfering with the process.

Anna was right. She knew it and I knew it. With about four or five hours of uninterrupted instructional time, Anna could be an independent user of a machine that offered her some independence. I couldn't lie and deny what she had just said. "Anna, you're right. But this is the way schools are: when the bell rings you are scheduled to be with Ms. Bennette for math."

Anna continued her protest. "But that's stupid! Don't they realize that it's more important for me to learn this than reviewing fractions?"

Without hesitation, I said, "Anna, sometimes it's hard for schools to take into account what individual children need to learn. There are many children in school, and schools have to be sure that all children are learning their basic skills."

"But can't they see that's so stupid?," was her next comment.

As I began clearing the table I said, "Anna, it probably is stupid because we need more time and can't get it right now, but unfortunately that's the way it is. If I could change things I would, but for now we're both stuck with it and you must go to class while I go off to meet with some of your teachers." Anna hurried off and I went about my duties. But I was troubled by her clear understanding of the "stupidity" of the rules, and by my inability to give her the attention she so clearly needed. Just as bells interrupted significant learning for Anna, other children were thwarted in their strong desire to know things not taught in the traditional curriculum. These students resorted to extraordinary means, like undercover reading, to obtain that knowledge. I once thought that students who hid books below desktops or behind textbooks were avoiding learning. Now I began to see things in new light. For the most part, such children were good students. In fact, they epitomized Holt's point that children want to learn and are capable of doing so without school or teachers. Unauthorized reading generally took place when lessons bored these students; they read literature or worked ahead in their math, history or science books. Ironically, they had learned that they had to conceal their interest in learning!

Other children had to pursue their interests after the three o'clock bell had rung. Just as I once had thought that children who read unauthorized books were avoiding learning, so too had I been misguided about children who loved to participate in sports, art, music and theater. Now, as I read through the pages of *Growing Without Schooling*, I could see that children who loved athletics and the arts were also pursuing knowledge. Even after a long day at school, these youngsters were motivated to learn. They epitomized the self-directed learner.

My views about school were definitely changing. I came to believe that even disaffected older children wanted to know more than I had previously thought. From my new vantage point, it seemed obvious that their natural cravings for knowledge left most schooled children with only one alternative: to find time on their own to do things that were important to them. I wondered whether Christian might some day find himself in the same boat. We knew he could adapt to school, but I couldn't help wondering how this might affect his sense of self-worth. We asked ourselves what the long-term effect of such experiences might mean for our son.

Socialization: the entire spectrum

Many parents who wrote to *Growing Without Schooling* expressed concerns about children's socialization, in both school and home. For many, inappropriate or detrimental socialization was why they decided to keep their children out of school in the first place. They considered socialization to be a much broader concept than simply teaching children manners or how to get along with one another; rather, they saw it as helping their children develop a strong sense of their own self-worth. In their opinion — and in my own newly-developing consciousness — schooled children had little chance to develop such inner strengths and moral attitudes in a system that focuses on rules and regulations, and tolerates, or even fosters, quashing the spirit of children who don't fit the norm.

Until my summer reading made me more aware of it, I had not paid much attention to the kind of relationship that schooling fosters between children and adults. In particular, it had not occurred to me that when adults take over the learning process, children tend to feel inferior and this casts the adult as the "enemy." Was this an attitude we wanted to foster? David and I knew that our preschooler, Christian, enjoyed the company of adults and children alike. If Christian were to go to school, could he continue to develop such easy relationships with adults? I had witnessed a good example of how children view adults as the enemy as part of my work with Anna. I attended some of her math classes in the course of helping her learn new math symbols in braille. Anna and I had resigned ourselves to the fact that the students were very noisy. Some of the kids were disruptive, while others simply liked to talk. One morning when the chatter was interfering with Anna's ability to hear what her teacher was saying, she called out, "Hey, you guys be quiet so we can hear!"

Neither Ms. Bennette nor anyone else heard her. The noise continued. Finally, Anna asked me, in a rather irritated tone, "Who's doing that drumming?" In front of us, a young boy was absent-mindedly drumming on his desk while he worked. He appeared to be deep in thought, so I knew that he wasn't drumming to cause trouble. Quietly, I went to his desk and asked him to stop the drumming. Without a pause, the boy looked at me and said, "You're not my teacher, lady, so don't tell me what to do." Surprised by his defensive response, I calmly reminded him that Anna could only learn by listening. Continuing to glare at me, he said, "So?" He did stop his drumming, so I thanked him and returned to my place at Anna's table.

I was taken aback by his behavior. Although I had witnessed students being rude to teachers, administrators, and each other, I had never seen a student being rude to adult strangers. This young boy appeared to be well-mannered, and on days when I sat in class with Anna, he seemed to work quietly and never disturbed those around him. His response was completely unexpected. Had I offended him or crossed some personal boundary? I didn't have a clue.

During the course of the next few months David and I discussed this event and others like it more than a few times. Our discussions led us to conclude that neither the boy nor I could be faulted. What became clear was that, as class bells rang, and individual student needs were ignored, and adult lesson plans displaced students' initiatives for learning, children seemed to lose respect for those who foisted such disruptive and meaningless routines on them. This boy's reaction to me probably was, we thought, an expression of an accumulated frustration with such treatment. If his needs were not being met by his math teacher's lesson, he was doing the best he could to make the situation bearable. Withdrawing from the class discussion, he had gone ahead with the assignment and absentmindedly began to drum on the desktop as he worked. When I had come to his side, all he could see was an adult who was probably going to interfere with his efforts and interrupt his train of thought.

Could it be that after spending years learning how to cope with a system that continually frustrated his own methods of learning, this boy could only see me as the "enemy?" Was this the future of Christian's relationship to adults?

As I continued to think about this, I finally understood how "socialization" encompassed much more than just peer relations. What about relationships with adults? In school, where teachers are in total command of the learning environment, children have little opportunity to develop relationships of mutual respect. What opportunity was there for a healthy relationship to develop when teachers controlled whether or not a child could get a drink of water, could use the restroom, or could study science and other pursuits in real life, rather than from a text book? When teachers restricted learning to only what their lesson plans called for, rather than allowing students to explore as they wished, were we really socializing children to believe that adults were there to help them learn? Were they socializing children to think of themselves as self-motivated learners and worthy citizens, or as inferior students waiting for instructions and believing that their own interests and questions were unworthy?

We thought about Christian's blossoming relationship with our community librarian, Roger. When Christian had questions that neither David nor I could answer, we'd make a mental note of the question and be sure to ask Roger to help us find the answer the next time we were at the library. As we modeled this behavior, Christian began to ask Roger questions himself. Soon this became part of Christian's library ritual. It was a treat for him to go to the library with a question for Roger and then go with Roger to find books that answered it. Fortunately, Roger understood the importance of letting children's natural curiosity lead them to the answers they sought. If Roger had told Christian what books to read or assigned a specific number of pages to be read, Christian would have lost interest. This sort of "teaching" would have undermined Christian's developing sense of himself as an able learner worthy of making personal choices about what was important to know.

As we reflected on what was most meaningful about socialization, David and I decided that Christian's opinion of himself should be our paramount concern. All that I had seen and experienced — the frustration of the boy drumming on his desktop, the bells dictating the beginning and ending of class, the security guards monitoring halls, the locker searches, the closed-circuit TV cameras in hallways and on buses, the limited access to lockers, the restrictions on recess activities, the restrictions on when students could attend to their own personal hygiene, and, most shocking to me, the requirement for *silent* lunch periods — made us wonder whether school could be a positive experience for Christian.

Although many of these conditions were a result of the need to assure safety and manage large numbers of children, their effect was to estrange children from their natural curiosity and desire to learn. Bells marking off segments of the day only served either to interrupt a child's rapt immersion in learning — or to provide a welcome relief from boredom. Security guards and locker searches gave a sense that school was not a safe place. Closed-circuit TV cameras engendered a sense of distrust between students and adults. Limited access to personal property in lockers deprived children of the opportunity to manage their personal belongings and their free time. Adult regulation of children's personal hygiene needs ran counter to expectations that children develop independence in their personal care. Silent lunch periods deprived children of the chance to enjoy the company of their friends at meals.

David and I were pretty confident that we could keep Christian connected with his playmates; but could we keep him connected with his growing need to discover the world and become integrated with the adults in his life? We had our doubts and worried that if Christian went to school, he might some day become another frustrated and rude "drumming boy." Christian was now four, and as I cradled his newborn sister, Georgina, in my arms, I realized that in no time at all both of them would be heading out the door to kindergarten. Homeschooling seemed to be worth further investigation.

⚜ Chapter 3 ⚜

Small Beginnings

"Children who come to school reading just cause trouble in the end."
— *Supervisor of student teachers, St. Paul*

As I fastened Georgina into her car seat, Christian asked, "Mom, will you put my new library books on the seat so I can reach them?" Reaching across the stick shift, I fumbled until I found our bag of books and then passed them over my head back to him.

For the next few minutes, the car was silent as we drove through busy downtown traffic on our way home. Then I heard a little voice say, "'Hop, hop went the little frog. Hop, hop, hop, went the big frog....' — Mom, what does s-p-l-a-s-h spell?" Inattentively, I answered, "splash." His little voice continued on, "'Splash, splash went the little frog. Splash, splash, splash went the big frog. The little frog and the big frog went ....' — Mom what does s-w-i-m-m-i-n-g spell?" Again I answered, "Swimming." Almost as soon as the word "swimming" was out of my mouth, Christian continued, "'in the pond.'"

As I tuned into what was taking place in the back seat, I realized that Christian was actually reading! With only occasional questions about words he saw on signs, labels, and in stories we read to him, he had figured out enough about the process of reading to read a story about imaginary frogs to himself. As in times past, Christian had taught himself one of the most difficult life skills and once again I was struck by his innate abilities. It was then that I began to seriously wonder whether we really had to send our children to school.

With Christian's fourth birthday, David and I began having more serious discussions about homeschooling and self-directed learning. Though we both felt that learning at age five was no different from learning in any of the previous years, we were unsure about what might be in store for Christian at age six, twelve, or seventeen, if he didn't go to school. Would he keep his strong appetite for learning? How would Christian or Georgina fare learning at home and from the community at large? We didn't yet know any homeschooling families and we felt adrift. With all of this, I began to see that my work as a teacher was becoming a contradiction to my life as a parent. As an educator, I had been trained to believe that my teaching skills were necessary for children to learn, but as a parent, I had come to believe that children had a natural desire to learn. As a teacher, I worried about our children not getting a full education, but as a parent, I had become confident that homeschooling would benefit our children. With all the hours of observation and all the reading I had done, I was in a better position than most parents to see the advantages of homeschooling and the disadvantages of traditional schooling, and yet David and I harbored doubts about what to do.

We recognized that many idle and boring hours were spent in classrooms — but life at home could also be idle and boring. If we chose to homeschool using the child-directed approach or, more accurately, to "unschool" our children, what if they became idle and bored? We knew nothing about what became of such children. All we knew was what became of many children who accepted the boredom and idleness imposed on them by their school experience: for the most part, they became functioning adults like ourselves. There was a comfort in knowing this, but were we willing to settle for second best for our children just because it was comfortable? John Holt's books had piqued our interest in homeschooling. He had given us reason to doubt that trading in Christian's self-motivated education for a life controlled by bells, teachers and standardized curricula was going to put our minds at ease. We had been introduced to the exhilarating possibility of bettering the lives of our children and we couldn't let it go without serious consideration.

Two self-taught readers

As David and I became more serious about homeschooling, Christian continued learning. While re-reading my journals about Christian's development, I noticed a pattern:

November 7, 1980 — Today, when reading to Christian, he asked me, "Where does it say 'Pooh?'"

December 2, 1980 — Christian asks me to point out certain words as I read to him.

July 19, 1981 — Today, while I was cleaning the bathroom, I asked Christian to read me a story. I have never asked him to read to me before. At first, he spoke gibberish but then he "read" to me, using the pictures to help him tell the story. Later at bedtime, he did the same with a library book. Going from front to back is a little confusing to him but he got the idea after a while. He remembered the detail that went with each page and did a great job. He is presently asleep on his bed in a pool of books.

August 25, 1981 — Lately, Christian has been asking a lot of questions like, "What does 'dog' start with?" Sometimes he gets confused and asks, "What does 'p' start with?"

October 11, 1981 — Today, while playing in his room, Christian started repeating: "'n', 'o', 'no'." Earlier in the day, I had shown him a "No Parking" sign and told him what it said. I wonder if he remembers my orally spelling the word "no"?

October 21, 1981— Christian read the word "no" today. I had put a sign up saying "no sweet" to remind myself not to put sweetener on our breakfast. He asked, "Does 'n' 'o' say 'no'?"

January 9, 1982 — Christian has mastered another sight word. The other day he somehow learned the word "street." When it is with other words in a story, he can identify it. Now he can identify, "Christian," "street," and "no."

September 22, 1982 — Yesterday, at lunch, Christian was looking at notes I had written for the co-operative day care meeting. I had written "Chris McKeene," and Christian said, "Hey, that's part of my name," pointing to the "Chris." He reads more than we know but doesn't like to sit down and be "taught" or try to find words he knows when we ask him to. He also hates "school books" I have. I'm not sure what to make of it all.

By the time he turned five, Christian was really beginning to read to us. The process was so natural we almost didn't recognize what was going on. Christian simply began to read books. When he got stuck on words he was unfamiliar with he would call to one of us, "What does ..... spell?" He would continue reading until he found another difficult word and again would ask, "What does ..... spell?"

As I became aware that Christian was learning to read — in the back seat of our old Honda, on the living room couch, or while sprawled on the bedroom floor — I thought of Corrine, the little kindergarten girl who had joined my first grade reading group when I was a student teacher.

Corrine was a self-taught reader whose mother had insisted that she be allowed to participate in reading groups suitable to her reading abilities. After she had been in my first grade reading group for a short time, it was quite clear that even my group was beneath her skill level. I suggested to Ms. Jackson, my supervising teacher, that this young girl be put into a second or third grade reading group. This upset Ms. Jackson, who said firmly, "No." Confused by her reaction, I asked for an explanation. She asked whether or not I realized that school was not geared to meet such demands. Then she told me that if Corrine were moved two or three grade levels ahead for reading instruction, there would be nothing but problems: problems scheduling, maintaining correct class size and grade placement. Of course, this *was* a school, so these problems were understandable. But what completely confused me was her final comment: "Besides, children who come to school reading just cause trouble in the end." This statement baffled and irritated me. What sort of trouble could Corrine cause by being a self-taught reader? I was never given an opportunity to find out. Instead, I was asked to keep my reading group on track and not think further about Corrine's needs.

Now, as I thought about Corrine, I wondered if she had learned to read in the same way Christian was now teaching himself to read? If so, I felt sad that school might have gotten in the way of such a natural process. As I thought about this, I realized that David and I might be creating a problem for Christian if we continued to help him with his reading! As preposterous as this may sound, it was true. At work, I had heard teachers say, more than once, that parents who teach their children to read before the child gets to school cause the child and teachers problems. Although David and I weren't actively teaching Christian to read, I knew it made little difference: Christian was going to be reading by the time that he was ready for kindergarten.

As a teacher, I understood how having a reader in a class of non-readers could be problematic. Self-taught and advanced readers posed difficulties for reading teachers by interfering with pre-planned reading lessons. Corrine was a case in point. Although she was beyond the level of the first grade reading groups, teachers couldn't move her into the second or third grade reading groups because of conflicts with school schedules — and because of her young age. When I was told that Corrine couldn't be moved up, how was I to keep Corrine interested? She needed separate lesson plans tailored for her individual needs, but for already overburdened teachers writing extra plans for special students is nearly impossible. Teachers swamped with the tasks of classroom management need well-paced, structured reading lessons. But for students who have already learned to read on their own, such lessons only stifle their continued advancement. Teachers are unable to do much more for such students than allow them to quicken the pace of their work and to do lengthier written assignments. While this may keep advanced readers occupied, it usually does little to keep their interest in reading alive. Giving them "readers," or even trade books, and having them do work sheets will never be as motivating as the reading they are already doing for the sheer pleasure of discovery.

We could see that Christian's developing interest in reading might put him in just such a situation. He wasn't asking us to provide work sheets, vocabulary lessons, or phonics instruction. He didn't need us to turn each of his inquiries into a reading lesson nor did he want us to. Rather, he asked for more immediate and practical help. Should we continue answering Christian's reading questions or should we wait and let next year's teacher provide the help he was asking for? Realizing the absurdity of the latter choice, we continued to answer Christian's questions as he asked them.

Could school hinder Christian's desire to learn?

As Christian continued to teach himself to read, David and I came to understand that the pace of his learning was going to be set by *him*. Christian seemed to know what he needed to learn: if he asked, "What does 'c-o-o-k-i-e' spell?" — that's what he wanted to know. He had no use for us telling him, "Sound it out now. Look at the first part of the word. What does the 'c-o-o' say?" Such instruction only frustrated him. But if we had learned — from him — to refrain from turning his reading experience into a reading lesson, what would happen to him in school?

It was clear to us that Christian wanted to keep his learning free of restriction. We could see that his questions were important — and that they deserved our full attention. I remembered how I had failed to answer the questions of my young math student, who desperately wanted to know *why* she must learn to use the symbols ">" and "<" for "greater than" and "less than." We increasingly felt it our responsibility to do better for him than I had done for her.

When Christian was younger, David and I had helped him learn to tie his shoes, to eat with a spoon, and to play his records. He knew we had the skills to do such tasks and had willingly sought our help. Now, as a five-year-old, Christian was asking us to continue in that role. Just as he had asked us to help him learn to tie his shoes, he was now asking us to help him read. We could see that all of these tasks were part of the natural process of learning, and we recognized that we had already been homeschooling Christian and Georgina from birth.

We began to see that school created a false distinction between learning "really important things" and learning in general. For the preschool child, learning to tie one's shoes or to ride a tricycle are just as important as learning to read. Children make no distinction between learning one skill or another. They simply need to be allowed to learn when they are ready to do so.

As we came to grips with this truth, we had to consider our children's future. Decisions that we made now could have an enormous effect on their lives. In our effort to understand what might be in store for Christian, we worried about what might happen to him in school if he learned to read simple books during the summer before kindergarten. Would he remain happy and enthusiastic about learning?

Georgina learns to walk

Christian, like all children, was on his own trajectory. It was entirely different from the one Georgina seemed to be on. As we watched them both grow, we wondered how school could possibly serve them both equally well. Their learning styles were entirely different from one another.

Georgina, unlike her brother, sailed through the early steps of learning to walk. By the age of seven months, she could independently crawl to the top of the ladder on our small indoor slide. From that vantage point, she would look around the room and then back her way down the ladder. There seemed to be no limit to her physical explorations. Like her brother, she enjoyed climbing up and down stairs, onto couches, chairs, and even low tables. By the time Georgina was approaching eight months, she had mastered all the skills Christian had taken ten months to learn.

Up until this time David and I had naively expected that our two children would develop similarly. But, as Georgina appeared to be on the verge of learning to walk, we became aware of just how different she was from her brother. After taking her first steps, she returned to crawling. The ninth, tenth and eleventh months passed and still she didn't walk! Georgina had her own needs and somehow knew that she needed to spend more time crawling.

She seemed content on all fours. Unlike Christian, Georgina rebuffed our attempts to offer her a helping hand. She was quite insistent in her refusal to take our hands and allow us to walk her along. When she wanted to get from place to place via walking, she preferred using the table, chair or couch as her balancing anchor. Her preference for crawling remained paramount until she was a year old.

Watching Georgina learning to walk, I couldn't help but think of what might be in store for both of our children when they reached school age. If Georgina needed more time to master the skill of walking, what if she needed more time to learn academic skills? Would she be given such time? As David and I pondered this, we continued to question the basic assumptions of our educational system. We wondered about a system that expected all children to learn the same skills at the same time. We questioned whether parents and teachers ought to put children into pre-established learning tracks. As we watched Georgina learn to walk in an entirely different manner than Christian, we wondered how either of them would fare in a school system that was hard-pressed to accommodate students with different learning needs. It was definitely time to try and make connections with other homeschoolers.

We find a family that homeschools

In the *Growing Without Schooling* directory I found the name of a homeschooling family who lived an hour's drive from us. Mustering my courage, I dialed the number and asked for Margaret. After introducing myself, I told her I had found her name in *Growing Without Schooling* and wanted to talk and ask some questions about homeschooling. She was willing to talk to me, but only had a minute to spare. In that minute, she told me she had been homeschooling her teenager and her eight-year-old for a year. I was ecstatic. Finally, I'd made contact with someone who was actually homeschooling her children! I quickly made arrangements to call Margaret back later in the week.

That time seemed to pass too slowly. Finally, the day arrived and I called Margaret again. I began by telling her a little about our family and that we were in the final stages of deciding to keep our son out of school the following fall. Out of curiosity, I asked her what had made her decide to homeschool. She said she had been concerned about her eight-year-old, Peter, because he had been floundering as a reader in first and second grades. As a result, Peter had lost all interest in learning and was becoming a problem at home and in school. After giving the matter considerable thought, Margaret and her husband, Derrick, decided to take both their son and daughter out of school. Since their main concern had been to rekindle Peter's interest in learning, they started the homeschooling process by abandoning all academic work. They filled their children's lives with opportunities to play and relax.

As Peter began to regain his happy attitude, Margaret and Derrick took up reading aloud to him. Soon he was being read to for at least three hours a day. Neither Derrick nor Margaret attempted to limit the scope of what they read to him. They indulged his interest in comic books, novels, newspaper columns, children's magazines — just about anything that held Peter's attention. They read to him as they sat snuggled up on the couch, or in their bed, or sprawled on the living room floor. Sometimes he would build with Legos while being read to. At other times he might be enjoying his lunch. The setting for the reading sessions and the content of the material made no difference as long as what was being read captured Peter's interest and kept him involved.

Margaret and Derrick read to Peter in this fashion for six months. During that time they never asked him to read to them or by himself — and finally their loving patience paid off. Peter began to ask them to help him read. Margaret concluded by telling me that Peter had become a good reader, and she invited me to call again. In subsequent phone calls, Margaret shared more of her family's story with me. She told me about her older daughter, Lucille, and her pre-schooler, Jacob. Lucille was learning about nutrition and the work of midwives, both keen interests of hers. More importantly, though, Margaret reported that Lucille really enjoyed being home rather than having to go to school each day. She didn't miss the daily grind of class work and the pressure to be in the right social crowd. I felt reassured by these words. Margaret also told me that Jacob was benefiting from having his siblings at home with him. Simply by being with the older children, Jacob was learning many interesting things. He had been present while Margaret and Derrick spent time reading to Peter and seemed to gain a lot from that experience. When Lucille talked about the births she was able to attend, Jacob learned about childbirth. For Margaret, the best part of the homeschooling process was that Jacob fit right in and learned as readily as the older children did.

To be sure, most of what Margaret's children learned evolved from the children's own interests. One evening, as Derrick was preparing to take a business trip, one of the children suggested that the family go along. Although there was no time to make the arrangements for such a trip this time, Derrick made sure that on his next business trip, the family accompanied him. As far as Derrick was concerned, this was the biggest advantage of homeschooling. He no longer had to be away from his family for weeks at a time. They simply came along with him. Without school to attend, the children and Margaret were free to travel with Derrick. On these excursions, the family had the opportunity to learn about the history, geography and customs of the different regions of our country. They'd even had the opportunity to spend a month or more doing volunteer work with John Holt in his Boston office!

These conversations gave me the first real glimpses of what a homeschooled life was like. Margaret's stories reassured me that homeschooling provided numerous opportunities for socialization across wide age ranges and between many cultures. It became apparent to me that daily life offered many more and varied social opportunities to homeschooled children than to children obligated to be in the classroom seven hours a day. Even if our family could never afford "luxuries" like microscopes, kilns, or textbooks, our children were likely to have a more enriching experience learning at home and in their communities. After many conversations with Margaret, I finally felt as though homeschooling was an alternative well worth trying. David and I simply needed to find the courage to follow Christian's lead and continue to help him learn.

We find a homeschooling support group

Over time, Margaret and I became friends. Our homeschooling interests were similar. Like me, Margaret was inspired by John Holt and believed that children were best able to create a meaningful learning environment for themselves. As we got to know one another, I expressed an interest in meeting other people who had similar feelings about children and learning. Margaret told me she had been participating in a newly-formed support group for parents who were "doing school at home"; she'd found it comforting to sit in their circle and discuss children and learning.

I attended my first support group meeting and was graciously welcomed. The first order of business was to introduce ourselves and tell a little bit about our homeschooling experience. As the introductions moved round the circle, I was startled to hear parents describe their homeschooling situations as if their goal was to replicate traditional school rooms: with basement classrooms furnished as any school classroom might be; mothers and fathers functioning as traditional teachers using standardized curriculum, textbooks, worksheets and testing; and traditional class periods and recess periods. Margaret's use of the phrase, "doing school at home," hadn't prepared me for hearing this. As I listened, I wasn't sure if it would be acceptable for me to say that my intention as a homeschooling parent was the opposite, to rid my children of traditional constraints. Finally, when it was my turn to speak, I introduced myself as a teacher who longed to get away from the traditional teaching environment. I mentioned John Holt and said that he had inspired David and me to give homeschooling a try. A few parents asked me who John Holt was. With a few brief words, I told the group about his books and his newsletter. I was relieved when nobody criticized me for wanting to homeschool as I did. By evening's end, I realized that although the content of the discussion had been frustrating to listen to, I had felt welcomed and it would be worth my while to attend a few more meetings.

At the second or third meeting that I attended, a woman and her husband shared the story of how their son learned to tell time, read maps and calculate travel time as they drove across the country. The child was seven and had been bored with all the driving that their family vacation entailed. Both mom and dad had become tired of answering the age-old question, "How much longer till we get there?" In an attempt to quiet their son, they decided to show him that he was capable of calculating the answers to his questions himself. Showing him the map and the planned course of their journey, they demonstrated to him how he could locate destinations, read the mileage markers between their current location and their destination, and calculate the amount of time it would take to reach that day's destination. This captured their son's interest. For the duration of their vacation, he kept a log of the miles traveled, hours spent traveling, gas consumed, gas mileage and other interesting facts. As the log developed, these parents realized that they might never have discovered that their son was capable of calculating such complex math problems had he been enrolled in school. During the year their son had been in kindergarten, they had left all of the "teaching" tasks to the teacher for fear of doing wrong. Now they felt empowered and capable of helping their son learn many things. It had been a "win-win" situation for everyone. Their son was delighted to keep a trip log and the parents had learned that they were quite capable of providing for their child's learning needs, whether or not it was part of any curriculum. This last point struck me. Here was a living example of parents who had learned to trust in their child's inquisitive nature and to "teach" from that perspective. If these parents could teach an inquisitive seven-year-old, surely David and I could do so as well. Listening to them tell their story helped me understand that helping Christian continue to learn would be as easy and natural as it already had been.

At a later meeting, I was to hear another story that encouraged me further. Mary's story was simple yet beautiful: how she learned to integrate her children into her life. When Mary's children had been in school, she had never felt inclined to include them in the everyday tasks she had to perform as a parent. When she sent them out the door to school, she "sent them out of her life." When it was necessary to take her children with her as she ran errands, she failed to include them in what she was doing. Soon, her children began to constantly complain as they followed her to the library, grocery store or pharmacy.

After making the decision to homeschool, Mary's attitude toward them changed. When they complained about having to tag along on errands, or demanded attention as she tried to prepare meals, she reconsidered their situation. She had begun homeschooling the children because she wanted to be more involved with them. Now Mary realized that she had to offer them more opportunities to join with her in the day's activities. She started this process in simple ways. When she cooked a meal, she found ways to include her children in the activity. As Mary planned meals, she encouraged them to skim the pages of cookbooks and suggest recipes that they felt might be good to try. When she had to run errands, now she made an effort to do so when her children weren't tired and irritable. When she shopped, she included her children in the process by showing them how to do comparison shopping and talking to them about the nutritional value of fresh foods. After having spent years of unintentionally excluding her children from the routines of family life, Mary was rediscovering the joy of being with her children. She hadn't experienced such joy since her children had been preschoolers. As I listened to Mary talk, I was moved. She was talking about discovering the joy of living with one's children, as I had never heard it expressed before. I understood that even if this were all that homeschooling would provide, it would be well worth it.

Meeting a real live teenage homeschooler

Although all of the stories I heard parents tell in our support group meetings were inspiring, I still doubted that such wonderful things were *really* possible. I must not have been the only parent with such concerns, because at one meeting a woman volunteered to ask her seventeen-year-old son to come and talk with us about his homeschooling experiences. This woman — a single parent no less — had been homeschooling her son for seven years. I awaited the next month's meeting eagerly.

Her son, Stephen, appeared at the next homeschooling support group meeting. Without hesitation, he sat down, introduced himself, and began to tell his story. Stephen's mother had withdrawn him from school as a ten-year-old. During his first years at home, Stephen had followed a strict traditional curriculum, using a correspondence program. During the academic year, he remained active in sports and in the summer he enjoyed camp experiences. As Stephen got older, he decided against continuing the correspondence program and chose to plan his education with the help of his mother. Each year, they looked over textbooks, study guides and library materials in order to plan an interesting course of study. After picking an assortment of materials to use, they decided what needed to be accomplished in each subject area. From this point on, Stephen's mother let him decide how to achieve his goals. She was always available to help him, but she didn't dictate the hours of study or the topic of study. When he felt the need to work, he worked; when he felt the need to play, he played. Stephen told us he was entering Junior College in the fall; it was apparent that he had managed his time and studies well.

Although much of Stephen's education had been based on traditional notions of schooling, he had been allowed to step out of the mold from time to time. His mother had encouraged him to participate in local political events when he was interested in doing so. At the end of one of these ventures into the world of politics, he felt the urge to "bring closure" to his work. To do this, he wrote a 30-page paper summarizing his experiences. Although David and I were not considering using textbooks, I appreciated hearing how this young man had been given the freedom to weave both traditional and non-traditional schooling methods into his life. His mother trusted him to know what he wanted to learn and had set him free in the real world of political activity. Her ability to sense his need to explore politics had given him a rich life experience.

When Stephen finished summarizing his experiences, he asked for questions. A concerned father, after hearing that Stephen had been given full responsibility for deciding when to work and when to play, asked Stephen whether or not he had difficulties "keeping up with his studies." Stephen answered this man's question by saying that it had been no problem for him. He then proceeded to tell us that, when he was fifteen, he had difficulty studying math. Although he had selected a textbook with his mother, and planned what he wanted to cover that year, he couldn't bring himself to start work on it. Instead, he felt a desire to be outside, and so he began to split, haul and stack wood for the family's wood stove. For two months he chopped and stacked wood — and then he felt like he wanted to start working on math again. When a parent asked him why he felt this urge to return to his textbooks, Stephen said it was simply an urge he felt, an urge to settle down to doing some math. He said his mother hadn't badgered him either to chop wood or to study math, and for this he was thankful. Stephen summed up by saying that he completed his math studies by early spring, in time to be outside once again!

Stephen's was the story that moved me the most. If a young teenager could manage his own studies, anything was possible! I had read about such self-motivation and now here, in the flesh, was a boy telling me that when children are trusted to learn, they will — and they will do it on their own without prodding from well-intentioned adults.

As I listened to Stephen I was transfixed. He seemed to make all my doubts evaporate. Here was an articulate, well-mannered young man who was comfortable speaking to a group of unfamiliar, inquiring adults. He never once displayed a lack of self-confidence, even when our questions were rather blunt and challenging. Stephen and his life story finally convinced me that David and I had nothing to lose by giving homeschooling a try. (Little did I realize that my son and daughter would later be giving similar talks to curious parents and students!)

David finishes his degree: what next?

As I began attending these homeschool support group meetings, David was finishing his Ph.D. With its completion, he would be looking for work. We were sure that a job for David would mean a move for our family and probably unemployment for me. This confluence of events, and the fact that Christian was now five, seemed to offer us the perfect opportunity to give homeschooling a try — and we decided to take the plunge.

Chapter 4

Our First Year

A Walk Past Ellen's House

One day, a boy named Toby was going to walk past Ellen's house. Just then the other boys on the street walked past. Toby got up and he walked past Ellen's house. Ellen was not home, so he said to himself, "I'll see if she can have company later." He went back to his house and just as he got into his house the telephone rang. It was Ellen, asking if he could come to her house. He said, "Yes," then he went to ask his mom if he could go to Ellen's house. His mother said, "Yes." Ellen was waiting by her door for him to answer "yes" or "no." He said, "Yes." She said, "Wait there for a second, I have to go ask my mom and dad if you can come in to play." Next day, the same thing happened. Ellen called Toby to see if she could come to his house to play. His mother said, "Yes." She walked down the street to knock on Toby's door. He let her come in and he asked her what she wanted to do. She said, "I want to play Dungeons and Dragons." He decided to be a dragon. She decided to be a princess running away from home. The End.

— A story dictated by Christian at age 5.

IN JUNE OF 1983, A WEEK AFTER THE ACADEMIC YEAR HAD ENDED, David was offered a post-doctoral fellowship in Madison, Wisconsin. There was no question whether he would accept the job. I resigned from my teaching position and began thinking about the upcoming move and what it would mean for our family. David and I asked ourselves, once more, whether or not we were ready to take the leap of faith that unschooling our children seemed to require. Although my evening with Stephen had shown me that homeschooling would work, David and I now had to consider the legal aspects of homeschooling. We knew nothing about Wisconsin law on the subject.

Researching Wisconsin homeschooling law

As our plans for the upcoming move solidified, it became clear that we would be leaving Minneapolis after the start of the school year. We were concerned, because we should have enrolled Christian in school or filed papers for homeschooling. Registering as "official" homeschoolers in Minnesota for the three weeks we'd be in the state seemed a waste of precious time. Since we'd followed suggestions about avoiding preschool screening and not talking to school census workers when they called, we felt relatively sure that any official who suspected that we had a school-aged child wouldn't find us until we were on the road. In the meantime, we had our work cut out for us. We needed to find out about the home-schooling laws in Wisconsin.

My most immediate source of information was Margaret, whose husband had family in Wisconsin. I called her in hopes that such a connection would provide me with some information about Wisconsin law. Luckily for us, Margaret had lots of information to share.

According to her, homeschoolers in Wisconsin had to have curriculum approved by the Department of Public Instruction before being given a legal go-ahead. Margaret wasn't sure, but she thought there was also a requirement for annual standardized testing. This was distressing news. Neither David nor I wanted to use curriculum. The whole purpose of homeschooling, as far as we were concerned, was to let our children learn in an environment free of curriculum, and free of standardized testing. As I expressed my concerns, Margaret consoled me by saying that we might "hide out."

I knew what "hiding out" meant. I'd read about families in *Growing Without Schooling* who had done just that — going underground. Although David and I planned to evade the Minnesota requirements for the short time we would be in the state, I honestly didn't think we could or wanted to remain underground indefinitely nor did I think that it was possible to do so in the midst of a city like Madison. I thanked Margaret for her information and with a heavy heart turned to the pages of *Growing Without Schooling* for further solace.

In the *Growing Without Schooling* directory, I found a listing for *Network News*, a Wisconsin newsletter. I sent the editors a letter asking them all my questions about Wisconsin law and was happily surprised to receive, via return mail, a long letter of reply and copies of the most recent issues of *Network News*.

Hope was restored by one simple sentence: "Kindergarten isn't mandatory in Wisconsin." We wouldn't have to worry about enrolling Christian in school until he was six! What a relief! We'd be able to try homeschooling without having to worry about getting the approval of the Department of Public Instruction. We could keep Christian home and continue to assess whether or not we thought homeschooling was in his and our best interest, without having to worry about the authorities pounding at our door. If, at the end of this trial period, Christian seemed to need schooling, we could enter him in first grade. It all seemed too good to be true.

I was overjoyed to read in *Network News* that, at the moment, Wisconsin had no compulsory attendance law. In a significant case — State of Wisconsin vs. Popanz — the State Supreme Court had ruled that Wisconsin's compulsory attendance law was unconstitutional because it was "impermissibly vague." A homeschooling family had been prosecuted under the existing law, had appealed the court's decision to the State Supreme Court, and had won. The ruling stated that if students attending private schools were to be prosecuted for truancy, "private schools" had to be defined. At the time that decision was handed down, there were no statutes defining private schools, and therefore homeschoolers could no longer be prosecuted for truancy. With this bit of news in hand, it seemed that Wisconsin would be the perfect setting for our first year of homeschooling.

In September we loaded up a rental truck and our old Honda Civic and headed south for Madison. We were overjoyed to be moving to a state where we would be able to homeschool without restriction, for at least a year.

New state, new city, new apartment!

After arriving and unpacking some of our belongings, Georgina, Christian and I said good-bye to David — who had to return to Minneapolis to finish up graduation requirements — and began our "school" year. Although most five-year-olds would be sitting at the feet of their kindergarten teachers listening to the day's instructions, that Monday morning I intended to begin our first homeschooling day quite differently. The weather was so nice, I opted to take the children on a long walk to learn about our new neighborhood.

Within half an hour we found ourselves at a Goodwill Store, checking out the bargains. Georgina made a toddler's beeline for the stuffed animals, while Christian explored the games. I kept a close eye on both children as I perused the rack of snowsuits, trying to find one suitable for Christian. While shuffling through hanger after hanger of jackets and snow pants, I noticed a beautiful redheaded baby standing beside her stroller, who looked about Georgina's age. Next to her, holding the stroller steady, was her mother. We caught one another's eyes and started a conversation. As Melanie and I talked, her daughter, Emily, and Georgina discovered one another. We found we lived within walking distance of each other. Melanie and I exchanged phone numbers, gathered our respective children together, and agreed to call each other within the next few days. This brief encounter developed into a long-lasting friendship.

Christian, Georgina and I headed home, taking a different route, past a park and through the surrounding neighborhood. As we approached our apartment, I felt great satisfaction in knowing that Christian's first "kindergarten experience" had been one in which he had explored his neighborhood, found a deck of cards and two books for 75 cents, and got a good dose of fresh air to boot. This was a perfect start for our first homeschooling year.

In the days that followed, the three of us continued to explore Madison. Soon the rhythm of our days became centered in the life of our community. Weekly trips to the library, a free noon concert, a support group meeting for mothers of young children, involvement with the effort to establish good homeschooling laws in Wisconsin, and trips to the grocery store filled our mornings. Daily, we attended to the mundane tasks of life: dirty diapers, dishes to wash, dusting and vacuuming. On other days when there were neither excursions to take nor household chores to do, we simply spent time playing together. Our days were nothing like "kindergarten" — and yet Christian seemed to thrive.

Should we keep a low profile?

When we arrived in Madison, we decided to keep a low profile. Having experienced some disapproval when talking to some of our Minneapolis friends about homeschooling, we decided it would be best not to discuss school issues when meeting new friends. In our new community, we didn't want to alienate anyone. Rather, we wanted to make connections with people as quickly and easily as possible.

Within a few months, we developed a wonderful circle of companions and Christian and Georgina had become friends with the many children who lived in our apartment complex. As we met our new neighbors, people would ask how old Christian was. When we answered, "He's five and a half," this response usually generated questions about kindergarten. We avoided raising eyebrows of potential new friends by simply answering that Christian would begin school in the coming fall.

Soon after settling into our small apartment, David and I began subscribing to *Network News.* For the next few months, it was our sole source of information regarding homeschooling law in Wisconsin. Reading the newsletter, it became clear that we'd have to get politically involved if we wanted to protect our freedom to homeschool. The new legislative session was about to get underway and it appeared that the Department of Public Instruction was pushing for restrictive homeschooling laws. It looked like we might lose our freedom to homeschool unless we joined forces with other homeschoolers throughout the state and lobbied for our rights.

As soon as we indicated our interest, our phone began to ring off the hook. The editors of *Network News,* Chris and Sue, who lived in the northern part of the state, wanted to know if they could rely on us to help with the lobbying effort. I wasn't sure how helpful David and I could be, given our limited mobility, but we offered to help in any way we could. After many hours on the telephone, it was clear that Chris and Sue had to come to Madison to continue their work. David and I offered them — and their three children — space to roll out their sleeping bags. That week, thousands of homeschoolers descended upon Madison, all mobilizing to lobby for the freedom to homeschool.

We make the headlines

Keeping a low profile was impossible once we became involved in the lobbying process. As the lobbying effort at the capitol grew, the local news media became interested in the story. A newspaper reporter was looking for a family willing to be interviewed, and we were asked if we were interested. Although the idea of being able to express my views was exciting, I was a bit skeptical about my abilities as an interviewee. I wasn't sure our family had much of a story to tell, nor was I confident that we could accurately report the details of the lobbying activities that were going on at the capitol, much of which were new to us. My homeschooling peers assured me, however, that the newspaper was more interested in reporting the "inside story" of homeschooled life than in the political events of the day.

That evening, I told David about the impending interview. Although we were both excited about this opportunity, neither of us had experience with the press. What had we gotten into? Would the reporter be friendly or hostile? How much did we dare say about the structure of our homeshooled day? All of these questions tumbled into our minds as we tried to discern how best to handle ourselves. In the end, we decided that, if indeed a reporter did contact us, we'd do the interview together. Together, we could support one another in case the reporter had a hostile attitude.

Sure enough, a reporter called the next day. We arranged to meet him at our apartment the following morning at 11:00. At the appointed time, the reporter knocked at our door. Behind him stood another man holding a tripod, with huge bags of photographic equipment hanging from either shoulder. We hadn't expected a photographer, but warmly welcomed them both. The reporter turned out to be more than friendly; he was keenly interested in our family's attitude about schooling and seemed to understand our philosophy of education.

But after about 30 minutes, he asked us to pose for a picture with me "teaching" Christian. Here was an illustration of just how difficult it was for people to grasp this idea of homeschooling. We'd just explained that we didn't sit down with books and instruct our children, and yet that was how we were being asked to pose ourselves! I again reminded the reporter that our children directed their own learning and offered instead to pose with them as we played a game together. That afternoon, Christian, Georgina and I had our picture on the front page of the local paper!

The accompanying story "blew our cover." We were no longer low-profile homeschoolers — and as we thought about it, we were happy about it. I discovered that the newspaper coverage provided me with the shot in the arm I needed to continue the tiring work of lobbying for good homeschooling laws. As a result of our collective efforts, within a short time the Wisconsin legislature passed a very favorable law guaranteeing our right to homeschool as we chose — without required testing, approved curriculum, or intrusive monitoring by the Department of Public Instruction!

A favorable law is passed — now what?

After this whirlwind of activity and its happy result, David and I turned our attention to whether to send Christian to school in the upcoming year. It had been easy for us to homeschool the preceding year because kindergarten wasn't mandatory: now we had to make a "real" decision. Would we register Christian as a homeschooler, as required by our new law, or would we enroll him in our local public school?

One evening, David and I sat down to consider our options. What we realized, as we looked back over the past nine months, was that Christian and Georgina had had a marvelous year together. Georgina had learned to talk with great fluency, while Christian had learned to read with ease. As we talked about their accomplishments, we remarked on what Christian might have missed had he been in school.

Although it seemed as if Christian's entire year had been spent lobbying with me at the state capitol, seeing the legislative process in action, he had actually done much more. He marveled as he watched his little sister acquire the budding skills of a two year-old. He built his own bird house, in the process learning how to draw building plans to scale, how to read a ruler and yardstick, and how to use a straight edge. When weather didn't permit working outside, Christian turned his building talents to construction with Legos, learning to follow detailed instructions and, when the mood struck him, to create his own Lego masterpieces. If Legos didn't interest him, Christian asked us to read to him. If we were unavailable to read, he pored over books that interested him, all the while teaching himself to read. When Christian's reading introduced him to weather forecasting, he became a "meteorologist," learning to read wind and rain gauges and how to graph his findings.

On Thursday afternoons, if Christian's forecasts predicted good weather, we all went to free concerts. At these concerts, Christian discovered he loved a wide variety of music. When he wanted to explore more musical avenues, we went to the library in search of new records and tapes to listen to. In the process, his knowledge of our community grew, and he met other adults who helped him find suitable musical resources, as well as more books to read.

As David and I thought about these wonderful accomplishments, we agreed that Christian would have missed a lot by having to attend school for a few hours each day. We concluded that keeping Christian home had been in his best interests. Now, we made the momentous decision to keep him home, officially, in the upcoming school year.

First-year doubts: are we doing the right thing?

As excited as I was at the prospect of being able to carry on as we had been, I still had doubts and concerns about homeschooling. I was still too new to unschooling to trust that we would continually experience success with our children. What Christian had learned in the preceding year had been a natural progression for him. As I projected my worries about unschooling into the future, I found myself thinking: would Christian naturally want to learn a foreign language at age thirteen? Would he take up algebra at fourteen, chemistry at fifteen, or many of the other subjects I thought were necessary to learn at particular times in order to survive in our complex world? With these thoughts still dominating my views of appropriate education, I had found it almost impossible to get beyond thinking about whether or not Christian was learning what he *should* be learning. In fact, such notions had been stumbling blocks for me during the entire course of that first year at home.

Throughout the year, I had been haunted by the "shoulds" of education that had been defined as the "necessities" of life. The "shoulds" were many: children *should* be able to write their name by age six, children *should* learn to add and subtract by age six or seven, children *should* be grouped with same-aged peers in order to become socialized, children *should* study biology when they are fifteen, textbooks *should* be used as the basis of study, children *should* be exposed to most of what it is important to know by the time they graduate from high school. Such thoughts often made me think about setting up a traditional classroom in our living room, but conversations with David about what it was we were attempting to accomplish as homeschooling parents kept me focused. Such conversations generally helped me clarify that Christian was indeed learning "necessary lessons" as he followed us to the state capitol, built his bird house, or played with Georgina.

At other times, my doubts about unschooling couldn't be overcome. On such occasions, I'd resort to the only things I knew: worksheets! I had a collection of them from my years as a vision teacher. Now with Christian of school age, but yet not in school, I used those phonics and number worksheets as my lifeline to the security I so badly craved. At my weakest moments, I'd dig out a worksheet or two and ask Christian to perform the tasks they required. The first few times I did this, he asked me why I needed him to do the work. Embarrassed by his forthrightness, I'd tell Christian I needed him to do the work because "children your age in school do this" and I wanted to be sure he was "keeping up." Christian had no idea about what went on in school but was willing to cooperate with his "teacher" when she expressed such a need. As the months passed, however, if I asked Christian to do more worksheets, he became less cooperative. He'd tell me how stupid the worksheets were and complain that they made no sense at all. I was always humbled by his clear understanding of the situation and would promise myself that I'd stop asking him to do such work — a promise difficult to keep.

On other occasions, when unable to keep my doubts about unschooling in check, I resorted to less-obvious means of checking up on Christian's learning. Sometimes this took the form of quizzing him on books we read to him or he read to himself. In my heart, I knew that Christian was learning from all that he was reading, but frequently, I was unable to trust myself and turned to assessing his progress in ways that I'd become used to as a traditional teacher. As with my worksheets, Christian seemed to see clearly the stupidity of my questions — and pointed it out to me! As before, I was humbled by his clarity of mind and would promise myself not to meddle.

Each time I resorted to the traditional school's means for assessing Christian's learning, I felt regret. Though I was now sure that unschooling was appropriate for our children, I found it hard to follow the unschooling path. When I talked to David about it, we realized the complexity of the situation. Here we were trying to create something, which we had never experienced — by relying on our past experience! Such a premise was flawed from the start. We realized that the only possible way to rectify our situation was to rely even more heavily on our children to show *us* the way. Through such conversations, we were slowly coming to understand that our concern that Christian might not be learning enough should focus instead on the *actual learning* that was taking place.

By year's end, we were not as doubt-ridden as we had been in the fall. Although we still found ourselves looking for evidence of learning as we were trained to think of it, we were less likely to fret when we found that Christian had learned about how bills became law rather than how to write his name neatly. We were learning that incomplete worksheets didn't indicate a lack of learning but rather a lack of interest in worksheets. Our discussions were making it clear that although we were far from a deep understanding of the essence of living the unschooled life, we were beginning to learn. Above all, we could see that Christian was learning, happy and healthy.

I start a homeschooling journal

As our first homeschooling year drew to a close, I began to keep a journal. Its purpose was to help me keep from meddling with Christian's learning while at the same time exploring ideas about schooling and unschooling. I found it quite comforting to use the pages of my journal to voice my doubts, and soon writing about my doubts became a source of discovery.

As the summer months passed and we readied ourselves for the upcoming year, I reflected on what I knew about schooled life and about Christian's first year as a homeschooler. "In school," I wrote, "a child's time in class is divided into segments such as social studies, math, reading, health, science, language arts, music, etc. These subjects are further divided into numerous 'units of study,' which focus on particulars of the broader subject. Reading might focus on biographies, math might focus on addition, and science might focus on geological formations in a particular area of the country."

As I wrote about Christian's self-defined "study," I made a remarkable discovery: hadn't Christian been doing "social studies," since he had been actively involved in the process of seeing a bill become law? In fact, the "unit of study" for his year had been "civics." And hadn't he also spent numerous hours doing "science"? One of his "units of study" had been weather forecasting. And reading, the subject that most kindergarten curricula focused on, had also been the main focus of Christian's year. Although I couldn't easily define what "unit of study" Christian had explored as a reader, I knew he had been reading in many different subject areas and had read both fiction and non-fiction. It appeared that his first year of unschooled life was just as rich as that of any schooled child — and maybe more so.

Family life as it really happens

Christian had also spent many hours living in, and learning about, a typical "family life" unit. I enjoyed writing about this in great detail: I listed the "units of study" that I knew might be included in school curricula — family structures, family relationships, life cycles, nutrition, emotional expression. If he had been in school, it was easy to see how Christian might have needed someone to "teach" him much of this material because being in school would have removed him from the natural source of such lessons: his own family and community life. As it was, Christian *experienced* the "curriculum" rather than had it taught to him.

For instance, Christian hadn't learned about how to care for young babies from books, videos and worksheets. Rather, Christian's *life expe-*

rience taught him that lesson naturally. Since he lived with his baby sister, day in and day out, he quite naturally learned about caring for Georgina as he watched David and me care for her. Likewise, had Christian been cut off from the broader community life he moved about in, he might have needed to read about single parent families, or families with disabled children, or families headed by same-sex parents, or families that came from different religious traditions and national backgrounds. As it was, his participation in the life of our community exposed him in a natural way to these and many other sorts of families.

As I wrote about these situations, I was excited to discover that Christian was easily and naturally learning material that professionally developed curriculums try to teach schooled children. More importantly, though, I was beginning to trust Christian's innate ability to choose courses of study that would be suited to his individual needs.

·⚜ Chapter 5 ⚜·

How We Learned To Homeschool

"The Moose"

Once upon a time there lived two charming children, Alison and Christian. They lived in the woods. One day they were looking for some berries when they found out that they were lost. As they went farther into the woods they saw a little shed. As they approached the shed they heard a loud groan. It was a moose. The moose was injured. They put a tissue over the injury. They made beds out of straw. The next morning the children woke up. The moose was gone! They looked all over the shed. The moose was nowhere to be found. They went outside. The moose was munching on some plants. The children were relieved. The children took the tissue off the injury. The injury was still bad but good enough to walk on. (Georgina, age 8)

IN THE EARLIEST YEARS OF OUR HOMESCHOOLING EXPERIENCE, routines in our household didn't change much. Georgina, still quite young, woke early, played vigorously, and collapsed for a lengthy afternoon nap each day. There was no time or need to try to impose a school-like schedule on a day so well-framed according to the needs of such a young child. Instead, we made conscious efforts to accommodate Georgina's needs, fitting our excursions into the community between her naps and bedtimes. One could say that our days were centered on the individual needs of our children and the interests they expressed. This was especially true when we first arrived in Madison.

Our first official year as homeschoolers

In late August of 1984, all the school age children in our apartment complex boarded the big yellow school bus and went off to school; all but one: Christian. David and I had finally decided, after years of thought and an experimental year of homeschooling, that Christian would fare better at home. That fall we were particularly excited. It was our first "official" year and we no longer had to pretend that we'd be sending Christian to school in the near future.

On October 15, David and I registered our first "Home-Based Private Educational Program" form with the Wisconsin Department of Public Instruction. This form, similar to the form all private and public schools filed, was simply a mechanism for taking a census of school-aged children. We were asked to give the gender and grade levels of all our school-age children and answer some basic questions: (1) Was the program of instruction to be provided by parents, or by a guardian, or by a designated tutor? (2) Was the primary purpose of the program to provide private or religious-based education? (3) Was the program privately controlled? (4) Did our program provide at least 875 hours of instruction each year? and (5) Did the program provide "sequentially progressive curriculum of fundamental instruction in the six mandated subject areas: reading, language arts, mathematics, social studies, science, and health?" We were also asked whether or not the program was "instituted for the purpose of avoiding or circumventing the compulsory school attendance requirement." After signing and mailing this document, we were elated. Our right to homeschool had been protected by law because of our own efforts and those of other Wisconsin homeschoolers.

That fall, I experienced a great sense of freedom. It was as if I had shed all the feelings of confinement I had felt as a child marching off to school. David and I looked forward with happy expectation to the months and years ahead. Christian and Georgina were now free to be at home, and could continue living and learning as they had been since they were born. The possibilities for their futures were almost impossible to comprehend. We simply allowed ourselves to experience the joy and the peace of mind it brought, and we let our life journey continue.

We meet homeschoolers in Madison

We began to look for homeschooling connections in Madison right away. In *Network News* and *Growing Without Schooling*, I discovered listings for two families who lived within commuting distance. One morning, while Christian was building with Legos and Georgina was playing an imaginative game with her stuffed animals, I called one of the numbers. The woman I spoke to, Donna, was the mother of four, one of whom was currently homeschooled; she and her child met each morning with other homeschooling families. As we talked, I knew I wanted to get to know her. She suggested that we join with all the homeschoolers in her group at the Civic Center for lunch and a free noon concert the following week. When we arrived, Christian and Georgina took an immediate liking to Donna and the boys who were part of the homeschooling group. That was the first of many regularly scheduled meetings together over lunch and music. Christian came to enjoy the company of the older boys and soon asked me if he could join them in their activities with Donna. So, on Wednesday mornings Christian began spending time at her home, while Georgina and I met elsewhere with a support group for mothers and their young children.

Our early homeschooling days

Such group activities usually played a key role in our morning routines. We would return home for lunch and naps. Afternoons were special times for Christian and me; with Georgina napping, we enjoyed a quiet time, napping or resting, and a change of pace from our busy morning routine.

Each day, after lunch, Georgina and I would retire for a period of quiet play, reading and talking. As her body slowed down, I'd lie down with her until she drifted off to sleep. In the meantime, Christian would finish his lunch, look at books, or play alone. After Georgina was asleep, I'd return to him and we'd enjoy a quiet hour or two together. Some afternoons, we'd do simple experiments from his chemistry set. On other afternoons, Christian might want me to help him type a story on our electric typewriter, or have me write down his stories as he told them to me. I frequently used this quiet afternoon time as an instructional period. Sometimes I would bring out the Cuisenaire Rods (small colorful rods used to teach mathematical concepts) and play rod games with Christian; sometimes we would read to one another from books that had caught our fancy. At the end of this time together, Christian would continue to play quietly by himself while I napped or rested. When the neighborhood children came home from school, he'd slip out the door to enjoy the rest of his afternoon playing with his friends.

By the end of our first year of homeschooling, this daily routine was well established. Although we never adhered to a rigid schedule, this was the basic pattern for our days. It didn't look much different from our days together before we had begun calling ourselves homeschoolers. The children's needs, and our needs as parents, were simply being woven together to form a supportive family network.

Music enters our life

David and I didn't intentionally set out to engage Christian in any particular activity in subsequent years. Rather, Christian's interests led him down unique and uncharted paths of learning. One of those paths was music.

As a four-year-old, Christian had the opportunity to watch Katherine, a ten-year-old, practice her violin. He was intrigued. Soon he started talking about when he'd be old enough to play the violin too. At first, we didn't give this much thought; but Christian continued to mention Katherine and to ask us for lessons. At the time, we couldn't afford to pay for lessons, so we told him, "When you are older and we live in our new home, then we'll think about violin lessons." This answer would momentarily satisfy him.

Maybe it was because David and I had to put Christian off, but for whatever reason, he soon became an *incessant* whistler. He whistled at the table, while reading, while playing with friends and while he pretended to be playing the violin. Although his whistling — of tunes both classical and contemporary — was remarkable, David and I felt as though we'd go mad listening to him; but we did our best to live with his homemade music.

Christian's whistling repertoire continued to grow each day. Luckily, I came across Nancy Wallace's book, *Better Than School,* and read the chapter titled "Music." In that chapter, Nancy related how her children had discovered music when her family moved to a house in which the previous owners had left an old upright piano. This made me realize that Christian's whistling and his interest in violin were things David and I ought to pay more attention to. Was it possible that his musical interests were pointing us to a new direction for Christian? David's new salary now made violin lessons possible; within a short time we found a Suzuki violin teacher who charged an affordable rate, and Christian began playing.

With the advent of violin lessons, our routines shifted. Christian started taking his private lessons during the day when the other Suzuki students were in school. He took his group lessons in the evening when his Suzuki peers were home. Clearly, as we'd expected, Christian was learning all of the time.

The group lessons with the other children came to be Christian's favorite part of violin instruction. For the next two years, he participated in any group lesson or group playing experience that he could. Unfortunately, just as he began his third year of violin, his teacher stopped offering group instruction, and she also discontinued having the children play for audiences in nursing homes. At this point, an interesting thing happened: almost immediately Christian asked to quit the violin. He told us, "It's no fun to just play music by myself; I want to play with others." It was clear that, for him, music was really a group activity, and unless he could play with others, he wasn't interested in continuing to practice. We tried to cajole him into keeping up his practicing, but Christian resisted. Eventually, we realized that his carefully-thought out reasons for wanting to quit were valid.

In December of 1986, Christian asked us to help him find a choir to sing in. Just as he had clearly thought about quitting violin because the lessons no longer offered opportunities to play with other children, so too had he clearly thought about why he'd like to sing in a choir. "Mom, in a choir there's no chance of not having people to play your music with. Please, Mom...?" Who could resist such a well-reasoned argument?

When I started looking for a suitable choir for Christian, somebody mentioned the Madison Boy Choir, a large choir with a national and international reputation. When I called, the woman I spoke with suggested that we attend an upcoming concert to see whether or not Christian would like to join. When I ordered two tickets for the Family Carols Concert, little did I realize that that one phone call would play such an important role in Christian's future.

On a cold and blustery December afternoon, Christian and I bundled ourselves up and went off to hear the Madison Boy Choir perform at the First Congregational Church. As the first choir stepped onto the risers, Christian was transfixed. After the first number, he whispered to me, "They're good, they're really good." When the second choir, the most advanced singers, took to the risers, Christian was beside himself with excitement. He marveled at the two boys who sang soprano descants above the 30-voice choir. As the choir left the stage to great applause, Christian begged me to let him audition. I promised him he could audition at the next opportunity. One month later, Christian was one of a small group of boys chosen to enter the training choir.

New experiences expand our horizons

In one way or another, we maintained the rhythms of our life as new learning ventures came our way — the rhythms just became more complex. By the time the Madison Boy Choir came into our lives, Christian had already integrated quite a few new activities into his young life. He regularly attended the homeschooling activities offered by our friend, Donna. In the fall and spring, he played soccer on a team that gathered at the park in our neighborhood. Once a week, David would work at home during Georgina's nap so that Christian and I could volunteer at the Mifflin Street Co-Op. It was here that Christian learned the meanings of "price per pound," "50 per cent off," and how to carefully handle the produce he packaged, weighed and priced for the co-op's shelves and coolers. While these activities were educating Christian, he was also developing many close friendships with both schooled and homeschooled children. His ventures into the community brought him into close contact with adults, many of whom he also considered his friends. Christian seemed to find a natural balance in his life as he took on more responsibilities, played with his friends and spent hours by himself reading books or playing with Legos and other toys. To us, he continued to appear happy, well-rounded and enthusiastic about learning new things.

Within a year of being admitted to the Madison Boy Choir, Christian met his personal goal of advancing through choir ranks to the highest choir, the Britten Choir. This choir traveled both nationally and internationally. At the time he was selected, plans were in the offing for the choir to tour Austria and Germany. The boys who traveled on this chaperoned tour would stay with Austrian and German families. This was a great opportunity, yet Christian had a concern: "How will I be able to talk to my host families if I don't know German?" He had a point. How could he get along if he couldn't talk to the people who would so graciously open their homes to him? We took his concern to heart and began to explore our options.

By this time, David and I were well versed in facilitating Christian's learning needs. When he had asked to be on a soccer team, we went to the soccer fields where he watched children play and asked a coach how Christian might get on a team. When Christian became fascinated with the workings of our local co-op, we asked the co-ordinators whether or not he'd be able to work as a volunteer alongside me. Finding a suitable choir had also meant asking around. By now, we were veterans at using friends, the Yellow Pages, and reference librarians as sources of help when Christian came to us with his questions. So, we asked our friends for possible resources for German instruction.

Through casual conversations, we'd heard a friend talk about foreign language camp experiences. Her children had attended language camps in Minnesota that taught Norwegian and French. Did they also offer German? Our friend told us, yes, there was a German camp, and gave us the address for Concordia Language Villages in Bemidji, Minnesota. Immediately Christian wrote them and asked for information.

Soon, a large packet of information arrived. Christian tore open the envelope, read its contents, and declared that "Waldsee," the German camp, would be a neat place to go for ten days. "They set the camp up as though you are truly living in Germany, Mom. We'll be issued a passport, and once we get to camp the counselors speak only German. The food will be German; we'll be using German marks for any treats we want to buy; they teach German songs and have classes three times a day." Christian's enthusiasm warranted giving the camp a try.

Our objective in sending Christian to Waldsee was to acquaint him with some basic German phrases; but when he returned from his ten-day stay, he was able to speak much more than that. In fact, he was so fired up about continuing to learn German, he wanted us to look for a tutor. Once again, David and I turned to our network of friends in hopes of finding a tutor.

Two days later, I was given the name of a neighbor, Sophie, who was German and had experience teaching children both German and French. This seemed too good to be true! I called her immediately and explained that I had a son who was homeschooled; I told her about Christian's language camp experience and how eager he was to continue learning German. We set up a time to meet, and two days later Christian, Georgina and I walked to her home for formal introductions. Christian and Sophie took an immediate liking to one another. By the time we left, we had set up a schedule for Christian to go to Sophie's two mornings a week for instruction. This was the beginning of a tutorial relationship that lasted three years. During that time Christian worked with Sophie and, in the third year with her, studied German at the local high school with her most advanced students.

As Christian's interests grew, our pocket book was shrinking. We had new expenses for soccer, choir (the tour would cost an extra $500), and German lessons. Christian was also begging for another stay at Waldsee language camp. Unfortunately, something was going to have to be given up. But this was unthinkable as far as he was concerned: "I'll earn the money for camp myself!" he declared. David and I looked at one another: how could we argue with such determination?

A month later, Christian was delivering a weekly advertising newspaper. He slogged persistently through wind, rain and snow in order to ensure his attendance at Waldsee. The paper route paid only $42 a month, which he knew wouldn't cover the $500 he needed for camp, so in order to earn more money he began to take on baby sitting jobs. Slowly, his bank account grew and as the time to send in his camp application neared, he realized, with great pride, that he would accomplish his goal. Not only had Christian worked hard to earn his way to language camp, he'd also worked many long hours at choir fund raisers, thus assuring that his costs for the trip to Germany would be kept to the minimum. This, too, gave him a sense of pride. He'd helped himself and his family afford the opportunities he so longed to participate in. The next year, he quit delivering the advertising news and took up a regular morning paper route, which he kept at for the next five years. This afforded him many more trips to camp and a second trip to Germany.

Georgina's interests take on a life of their own

By the time Christian had entered Boy Choir, Georgina had reached an age where she, too, had interests that beckoned her. Georgina was a much different child than Christian, and presented us with new challenges. Her most pronounced needs were to be physically active and socially connected.

By the time Georgina had turned five or six, homeschooling was becoming more accepted and this made it easier to respond to her needs. Four or five other homeschooled children formed the core of Georgina's active social life. I would arrange exchanges with the parents of these children so that Georgina might not only have friends over but also be a guest in her friends' homes. Such play opportunities offered Georgina a much-needed outlet to be both physically active and socially connected to children other than her brother, and she was happiest on these days.

When it wasn't possible for Georgina to have her friends over or to visit them, she entertained herself with wildly imaginative games. She'd bring stuffed animals to the living room, rearrange the furniture and play for hours in a magical world she created for herself.

Some days Georgina didn't feel like playing by herself at all. On such days she might come to me and whine, "I wish I was in school so that I could play with my friends." I knew from many conversations with her that Georgina's idea of school was a place where recess, lunch, art class, gym and music class constituted the main order of activity. Although

I understood her longing to be a part of this, I also knew what else school would mean for Georgina. Her special gifts were her talkative charm and her energy. If we enrolled her in school, we knew we risked repressing these qualities and losing the Georgina we knew, and subjecting her to the negative labeling schools often use. At home, Georgina's continual physical activity and lively imagination were seen as positive characteristics. In school, they'd be seen as "problems to be dealt with," and we couldn't risk that.

So when Georgina would ask to go to school, I would talk to her about what happens in school. Sometimes she would listen to me for a few minutes and then be off to play. At other times, she would persist and I'd indulge her by saying, "Let's play school, since we can't take you there today. Get some books and I'll be your teacher." Happy to play, she'd run off to get some books while I cleared some work space at the table.

When she spread her workbooks on the table, I'd look over the assortment and begin assigning pages for her to work on. All too happy to be playing a game, Georgina would quickly settle into doing the work I'd tell her to do. In my "teacher" role, I'd sit at the table and do some sort of paper work. Before too long, Georgina would begin to fidget and complain:

"Can I sit by the woodstove and do this. It's warmer there," she might say.

"Georgina, please raise your hand if you have something to say. You know the rules in this classroom," might be my likely rejoinder.

"Mom, stop being so weird. I just want to work in the living room. Can I?"

"Georgina, this is the second time I've had to remind you today about talking without raising your hand. If you interrupt again I'll have to put your name on the board and then you'll miss recess."

"But mom, this is just a game. This isn't the way it would be in school," she'd say.

I'd remind her that this was school, not a game, and that once again she'd spoken without raising her hand. This third "teacher like" response usually ended the game. At this point, I'd try to explain to her that, in school, children must sit where the teacher tells them to sit, that children must finish all their work before going out for recess, and that talking and moving about freely were not acceptable. Such comments usually intrigued Georgina, and I'd tell her a little bit more about school life before she became bored and decided that playing alone, or with Christian, would be much more fun than going to school.

The closest Georgina came to spending a day in school was when our friend, Donna, began offering classes in her home to homeschooled children ages five and up. The classes were very suitable for young active children: cooking, doing math, investigating foreign cultures, exploring the county park system, and the like. All of these activities included ample playtime. A day in Donna's home was ideal for Georgina: some structured activity and plenty of creative and physical expression.

Ever since her first birthday, Georgina had been enrolled with me in swim and gym classes, but when she turned five she was ineligible. However, she had become interested in gymnastics, and we thought that this would provide a suitable outlet for her physical energy. For the next two years, Georgina went to gymnastics class once a week and thoroughly enjoyed it. At the beginning of the next year, Georgina came to us with a new idea: "I want to quit gymnastics and join the swim team at the YMCA. It'll give me more exercise." Like Christian, who had explained to us the advantages of joining a choir, Georgina had carefully thought out her reasons for wanting to join a swim team. "At swim team, I'll get to swim two or three times a week and on some weekends." Both David and I had long recognized Georgina's paramount need for physical activity, but it was clear that she, too, was attuned to that need. Immediately, I looked up the cost of a "Y" membership. It fit within our tight budget and was actually less expensive than gymnastics. When I signed up Georgina for the swim team, I never imagined she'd be swimming competitively for the next six years!

Georgina also had a very strong affinity for animals. Besides housing a small menagerie of rats, mice, a bird and a dog, we did our best to nourish her interest in animals by reading about them to her, taking trips to various zoos, going on a whale watch (while in California visiting her grandparents), and enrolling her in various "enrichment" classes that dealt with some aspect of animal life. To this day, Georgina cares deeply about animals, and we expect this will be a life-long interest.

Our children choose well-rounded lives

During the ensuing years, our children's lives unfolded in quite natural ways. Christian's interests in singing and German continued to flourish, as did Georgina's interests in animals, social activity and physical expression. This is not to say that these activities occupied all of their time; rather, these interests formed an enduring thread, which was woven into the many things they did from one day to the next. During these years, David and I continued to hone our skills as learning facilitators and, over time, we came to understand the wisdom of letting our children be the guides in the learning process.

While Christian continued to study German and to sing on a regular basis, he found other interests, some of which were transitory, some longer-lasting. One winter he was an enthusiastic cross-country skier; he trained hard and participated in the state-wide winter games. But the next year, he skied for recreation only. At another time, Christian worked with Donna learning video production. This work included set design and make-up. Work with make-up soon became a deep interest. He intensively studied theater make-up techniques and became adept at creating amazingly strange (but believable) faces for actors. When this interest waned, he became interested in collecting comic books. After studying the artists and collector price lists, Christian invested some of his paper route earnings in valuable comics, thereby adding to the funds he could use for language camp, or touring with the choir. There was also a time when Christian made an intensive study of Greek art and then of Greek mythology. That interest led to some creative writing, about a mythical time and people. As these and other interests flowed through Christian's life, he continued to be actively involved in singing, studying German and community work.

Christian's first experience volunteering with me at the local food co-op had whetted his appetite to do more volunteer work. For a time, he helped at a local community meal program. When he wasn't setting tables or serving patrons, he'd work in the kitchen manning the industrial dishwashers. When election years rolled around, Christian always found ways to support candidates of his choice by doing phone work, helping with mailings and distributing leaflets. As he became more interested in the life of our community, he began volunteering at a local all-volunteer community-supported radio station. His experience with campaign telephone work was good training for answering the phones when the radio station's pledge drives came around, and he found other ways to be useful at the station. Soon he learned how to do pre-production work and how to engineer the board. As a result, he became an FCC licensed radio engineer.

At about this same time, Christian became interested in something completely different: on his own, he intensively studied the art of fly-tying and fly fishing. After doing this for four years, he was an accomplished fisherman and fly-tyer — and he had started a small, home-based fly-tying business.

All of these activities, and many lesser ones, gave Christian an authentic life which intimately connected Christian to his community and surrounded him with opportunities to continue his learning. In fact, by the time Christian was fifteen, his life was so much his own that David and I couldn't imagine thinking of him as a "student" or a "school-aged child." The natural course of his life had been well-balanced and had brought him graciously into the adult world. For Christian, there was no distinction between himself and the adults he worked with. For example, when opportunities to perform in professional choirs presented themselves, Christian, like any adult, simply auditioned for a place in the choir. When he wanted to expand his knowledge of German literature, he enrolled in classes at the university. If adult volunteers at the radio station needed to be trained, Christian was often asked to train them. This was not unusual, for Christian thought of himself as a peer of those with whom he worked. His participation in activities of the adult world had quite naturally transformed his concept of self from that of being homeschooled to that of simply *being*, simply living his real life. Christian's life was his *own*. As Christian says, "I'm not homeschooled any more; I'm beyond that, I'm simply *me*."

Georgina's life too, took on a flavor all its own. Although she was quite different from her brother, she too developed a few strong interests that seemed to weave naturally among the many activities of her life. Georgina has always needed a lot of varied social interaction, full of physical activity, and free of highly structured classroom routines. During summer months, she often participated in the enrichment classes that were offered by our local school district. Her favorites were classes in which she studied animals, pottery, cooking, and creative writing. After a morning of classes, she would ride her bike to a local pool and swim on the summer swim team. Some years, summer enrichment classes didn't entice her, but the activities offered at our local park did. When Georgina got older, she enjoyed attending YMCA camp. All of these opportunities provided her the social outlets and physical activity she needed.

As Georgina matured, she seemed to want to give some of her energy more purposeful direction. A naturally gifted singer, her interest in music had developed to the point that she wanted to begin trumpet lessons. But after a short while, her interest in trumpet waned and she decided that singing would be more to her liking. With such a strong voice and a love for performing, Georgina would be a natural for the Madison Children's Choir, and so we signed her up for an audition. Now, four-and-a-half years and two auditions later, she finds herself in the highest level of the choir, preparing for an international tour to Italy. As part of that tour, she auditioned for the World Children's Choir, and was selected to sing in its ranks. Given her affinity for new social experiences, she can't wait to stand next to children from around the world and make music with them.

Like Christian, Georgina has been quite active in community life. For years, she spent three days a week from noon until six at the YMCA. Here, she swam, volunteered as an assistant to the preschool swimming instructors, worked the front desk, and befriended the employees of the Y as well as developmentally-disabled patrons. Nowadays, she volunteers at the YMCA Annex, providing child care for preschoolers whose parents are attending classes. And, as if this weren't enough, Georgina also spends hours at a local family-run pet store. As a volunteer, she cleans the cages, waits on the customers, stocks the shelves, answers the phone, and sometimes works the cash register.

Georgina's life, at age thirteen, seemed to take on new and meaningful directions, like her brother's at a similar age. After devoting six years to her swim team, she quit to pursue acting. Currently, she studies acting, attends choir rehearsals, works at the pet store and at the YMCA Annex, and puts in countless hours of babysitting (she has to earn half the cost of the trip to Italy). She is also taking French lessons (in hopes being able to travel to a French-speaking African country in the distant future). As David and I see Georgina step out into this new phase of life, we realize that the days are numbered in which we will think of her as homeschooled. Like Christian, the community is truly becoming her school. Soon she, too, will be on a path that will take her into her *own* life with ease and grace.

A look beneath the shining surface

Although Christian and Georgina have successfully learned how to educate themselves, and have developed well-rounded social lives, it must be said that these accomplishments did not come without conflict. In the early years of homeschooling, David and I were very unsure of ourselves. We had no role model for what we were doing and no understanding that homeschooling is a lifestyle totally different from the schooled lifestyle. Without understanding this, we often found ourselves questioning much of what we were doing. In the beginning, when our doubts would get the better of us, we would revert to what we were familiar with — school "lessons." When I'd bring out the workbooks, both children would resist; this usually resulted in arguments and unhappiness.

Usually on these occasions, I would see that our troubles were caused by trying to impose school tasks on unschooled children; I'd then retire the workbooks and peace would return. But one winter, I found it particularly difficult to let go of my concerns, and this proved to be a turning point. The children seemed especially resistant to the academic lessons that I felt they needed. This resistance made me irritable and even more concerned that perhaps their education was suffering. Agonizing over whether we were doing the right thing, I finally called a local parochial school to inquire about openings for the following fall.

The principal, who was very kind, told me about her school, its commitment to maintaining small class size, her wonderful teachers and the courses that her school offered in reading, math, language arts, social studies, science, physical education, art, music and religion. As she described the course offerings, I felt a sinking feeling in my stomach. Then she told me she had one available opening for fall.

Hearing this, I suddenly realized that sending the children to a regular school was never going to be an option we'd seriously consider. When Christian was a preschooler, we'd decided against sending him to school because we thought it was the right thing to do for *him*. Now, as I talked to the school principal about my children, I realized that homeschooling them was more than a choice about education — it was the right thing to do for *us*. Homeschooling had become a way of life for all of us in our family. Enrolling our children in school would mean we'd have to surrender that lifestyle, and I knew in my heart that this wasn't an acceptable option. Although some days homeschooling Christian and Georgina could be taxing, they were just as much an integral part of our homeschooling life as were the more successful days. We could no more banish the kids on these days than we could banish winter days from the year. Learning to live with one another through rough times as well as good times was part of homeschooling. I realized that we had come to trust that our children's desire to learn would give them an education. I also saw that our children were giving *us* an education.

When I came to this realization, I began to experience the serenity that I'd been looking for. We let go of the fear that we weren't doing the right thing. From that time until this, unschooling has been something that David and I have been learning from our children. It has been a long and sometimes difficult process. Conflicts are still part of our everyday life, but are now about the more mundane aspects of our life together: doing the dishes, walking the dog, or doing the laundry.

Like all children, Christian and Georgina continue to need — and to resist — parental discipline. At times, we have had to withdraw privileges or impose firmly established rules. At other times, such conflicts have meant taking a closer look at family expectations. Establishing rules and boundaries, and modifying them as family needs change, is difficult, and yet is at the core of what we do as homeschoolers. In truth, it is not the study of this or that academic subject, but this interchange that is the essence of our life together as a homeschooling family.

As parents of children who have never been to school, David and I have learned a lot from the continual reshaping of our expectations to fit the individual needs of our children. Sometimes this learning went against the grain of everything we'd been taught in school. At such times, we found ourselves in conflict between our own deeply-imbedded beliefs about education, and our children's innate sense of how child-directed learning should proceed. Such conflicts spurred us into dialogue, and sometimes into argument. As we discussed our differences, we slowly built a path for our lives to take together. Maintaining a sense of discipline and family structure, while at the same time honoring our children's individual needs, has not always been easy. But, as we have learned to put aside our schooling-based expectations, it has become easier.

The whole picture

To this day, David and I are still challenged by the adjustments required by the ever-evolving interests of each family member. Although our life doesn't follow set time periods for the study of subjects, all subject matter is a vibrant part of our days. Natural science is a part of Georgina's experience as she works at the pet store; biology and ecology interest Christian as he studies trout, the rivers they live in, and the food they eat. Language arts are woven into both children's lives as they study a foreign language, write business or thank you letters, learn a part for a play, or sing in choir. Math skills and health education are part of both Georgina's and Christian's self-directed learning. Reading — a book, a magazine, or rules for a new game — is simply a part of everything each child does. Social studies is woven into their lives as they read the newspaper, discuss their parent's growing up in the '60s, watch election returns or PBS specials. They have both developed independent study habits, and often bring home library books on topics that interest them.

All of these things are part of the continual balancing and re-balancing of daily activities that have become the heart of our days together. We live, by choice, a life structured by its very real demands rather than by the artificial constructs of a school regimen. This lifestyle has its ups and downs; but when we consider our options, we know we're better off living this life that we have all chosen.

⁙ Chapter 6 ⁙

We Learn As Christian Learns

I am going camping in two days and David and I are going out west to a place called Spring Green. I hope you can fish there because I have been dying to go fishing ever since we went to North Carolina. I pretty much only catch seaweed, but ever since I saw people reeling in fish all day my hopes have lifted a little and now I feel that we will be able to catch some fish. If I do catch anything I am going to put it in some water and take a picture of it. I have only caught one fish in my whole life! I was taking a class on how to fish and the person had just taught us how to cast out and I saw the bobber bob under the water for a second. I caught the fish then.

— An entry from Christian's journal, October 15, 1987 (age 9)

Learning "write" from wrong

WHEN CHRISTIAN WAS FIVE he was eager to learn to write. To get him started, I purchased pencils, erasers, and wide-spaced blue-lined paper. Since Christian could already spell his name orally and say the alphabet, we began with these.

Unfortunately, printing "Christian" and the ABCs proved very difficult. He would reverse letters, such as "b," "d," "p" and "q," and even printed some letters backwards. The more instruction I offered, the more frustrated he became. I'd suggest he copy things from books, or copy things I wrote for him, or practice particular letters, or practice printing parts of letters that seemed to cause him the most trouble. Unfortunately, my methods only frustrated him further and Christian started to lose interest in writing.

What a disappointment! Here I was, a new homeschooling mom, full of self-confidence about improving on classroom instruction — and failing as a teacher in my first lessons! Luckily, Christian was still motivated to write. He would come to us for help when he wanted to leave notes for friends. He would ask us to take dictation when he wanted to write a story. He even continued to try, frustrating as it was, to follow our suggestions for learning to write.

But soon his frustration seemed to be getting the best of him. At this point, we decided to pull back and ease up to preserve Christian's self-motivation and ease the tension that was building up. We decided to let Christian show us the way to better help him learn to print.

This was the first time David and I felt challenged by the unschooling process. We had come to homeschooling not realizing that we had expectations of what children *should* do in order to learn traditional academic skills. Now those expectations were being challenged. During the course of the next few months, whenever Christian rejected my suggestions for helping him improve his writing skill, I'd silently say, "Show me the way," and try to listen, truly listen, to the underlying meaning of his questions.

We began to recognize that Christian had a clearer understanding of his problems than we did. For example, the paper that I gave him — typical wide-lined paper with a dashed line running between two solid lines — confused him. He'd never seen us write on such paper. When I realized that the lines on the paper were confusing him, I patiently explained how to place his letters using the two solid lines and middle dashed line as writing guides. It would be months before I caught on and realized that he simply wanted ordinary paper!

Christian had other frustrations learning to write. Often, he didn't know how to spell the words he wished to use, or how to use correct punctuation. These problems were somewhat easy to overcome. Because we didn't want to dampen his blossoming interest in writing creatively, we simply told him to write without worrying about such matters. If he wrote something that he wanted to share with others, we offered Christian our proofreading skills. This seemed to ease his concerns about writing for others to read.

A more difficult problem was that of "reversals." Like many children who are learning to print, Christian was apt to confuse "b" and "d," "p" and "q" and even write letters upside down. Christian was usually able to recognize incorrectly formed letters, but, unfortunately, this recognition often came well after he had completed what he was working on. This made him feel dejected about his writing. In the beginning, out of deeply-ingrained habit, I'd say, "Christian, with a little more practice you'll be able to write better." But as soon as those words were out of my mouth, I could see the expression on Christian's face change from being relaxed and happy to a look of tension and sadness. Silently I'd chide myself for not remembering to let Christian "show me the way."

One afternoon, about a year into these efforts with writing, Christian came bounding into our apartment, yelling, "Will you teach me cursive, Mom?" As he asked me this, he shoved a paper in front of me with the word "Chris" written on it. "Nicki taught me to write "Chris" in cursive and it's real easy. Please teach me the rest of my name." If this wasn't the perfect opportunity to practice "show me the way," I didn't know what would be.

Christian and I sat down to begin learning to write the rest of his name in cursive. Painstakingly, he worked on joining together the remaining letters of his name. We practiced together for about an hour. As I sat and watched him work, I realized how right it had been to let him show me the way. I was learning from him that cursive was much easier for children to learn than printing. No reversals were possible. The writing simply flowed from left to right!

A few months after Christian had mastered his writing skills using cursive, I was talking to a friend about Christian's discovery that cursive was easier to learn. She remarked, "If you look at the old McGuffy readers you'll see that all of the writing exercises, even in the earliest books, are done in cursive. Cursive was the first form of writing taught, but somewhere along the line a teacher thought that children should learn to print. One thing led to another and soon other teachers were teaching printing instead of cursive. But, as you've discovered, printing is simply too difficult for children to learn; it causes great difficulty with reversals and the like."

I ruin Christian's interest in his habitat study

When Christian wanted to learn to write, David and I initially failed to be of significant use as teachers. But Christian clung tenaciously to his desire to write, and finally, we grasped the idea of letting him show us how to be the teachers he needed. In this case, David and I realized we had to let Christian go at his own pace and in his own way as he learned to write.

Unfortunately this was not always the case. A few years later, when Christian was ten, he developed a keen interest in the nature preserve that is at our back door. During the winter months, he would ski the cross-country ski trails, and in the warmer months, he would just wander the acres. After one of these wanderings, he announced that he wanted to do a "habitat study." Apparently, he had been scouting for a plot of land to study for quite some time.

As on other occasions, Christian knew what he wanted to do and had devised his own plan of study. Over the next few weeks, he made repeated trips to his little plot of land in the park. Each time he returned from one of his excursions, he had new and interesting things to tell us. One afternoon he might tell me about a flock of geese that he'd seen heading north: a sure sign of spring! A week later, he might report that the temperatures were somewhat cooler; therefore some of the buds had ceased opening. His reports were always interesting and involved great detail.

In my eagerness to help Christian "do a better habitat study," I began to interfere. At my suggestion, he showed me his plot of land. It was simply a stretch of land next to the path, and included a piece of field, some low-lying shrubs, and a small section of woods. There was nothing particularly remarkable about it; it just was.

I, of course, being a "teacher" began to cook up lots of ideas about how he should do his study. I knew how such projects should be conducted! When I was in high school, our biology teacher had assigned just such a project, and later I had helped many of my own students put together science projects. These experiences called for the application of "proper methodology" and I was ready to see to it that Christian was well-versed in its use. Suggestions poured forth. I didn't bother to ask Christian whether or not he wanted my suggestions.

My first suggestion was that Christian measure his plot of land. Measuring, I surmised, would lend itself to creating a scaled drawing. I knew from experience that illustrations were an important part of any graded project and felt that Christian needed to include one in his work. Never mind the fact that he might come to the same conclusion on his own or, conversely, never feel that he should illustrate or share his work with anyone!

Christian acquiesced. Together with his sister, we took our meter stick (all scientific measurements must be done in metric measure — another of my "teacher" notions) and measured the plot. Without realizing it, I was already limiting Christian's project. Not only was I setting boundaries to something that he had seen as free of boundaries, I was also causing him to think in terms of my limiting experiences of "school projects."

When we returned home, I asked Christian to draw a scaled map of his plot of land. Christian saw no need for this but, like a good son, he tried. Soon his interest was truly on the wane. Seeing this, I once more attempted to take control in hopes of rekindling his dying interest in his habitat study. Before I had jumped in, I had noticed that Christian had been taking temperature readings using the thermometer outside our bedroom window. This met his needs. He simply enjoyed noting the temperature and the date and time of day that it was taken. Now I insisted that he chart and graph his readings, and, of course, this put a damper on his interest in keeping track of temperature at all. To counter this, I offered him a bribe — a nifty thermometer he could clip onto his jacket. Christian seemed to understand what I didn't; that the thermometer was not a gift, but rather an attempt to buy back his interest and that if he accepted the thermometer, he'd be more firmly bound by my notion of how *he* should conduct *his* project.

Although the thermometer temporarily rekindled Christian's interest in his habitat project, by this time the damage had been done. My schooled voice had overpowered Christian's intuitive idea of how to study his habitat, and as a result he gave up on it. Finally, as I watched him put away his notes for the last time, the light dawned; I remembered what John Holt had said in a *Mother Earth News* interview: that rewarding a child for work that is self-rewarding eventually kills the child's interest in doing the work at all. This was exactly what I had done. I felt remorse when I realized that my best intentions to help Christian had, in fact, not helped at all.

Reflections on failure

When I realized that we had effectively ruined Christian's habitat study, we sat down for some serious discussion. If we were going to continue unschooling, we needed to understand what had driven us to insist that Christian change the design of his study. Our discussions eventually led us to a truth that we were not readily acknowledging: in spite of our convictions about the merits of unschooling, we simply didn't trust our children and their intuitions about how best to learn.

Although we had watched our children initiate many interesting projects, any time Christian or Georgina decided to do something that reminded us of our school experiences, we'd feel the urge to help them "get it right." We'd meddle just a little bit with such projects, so that neither Christian nor Georgina would wander too far from our understanding of how things "ought" to be studied.

As David and I discussed what had happened to Christian's habitat study, we retraced the course of events. When he first told us of his plans, we were astounded. Neither of us would have assigned him such work. Initially, we had been content to let Christian proceed according to his own plans. There were days when Christian didn't work on his habitat study; other days, he was gone from the house for an hour or more collecting his data. Sometimes he recorded his data and sometimes he didn't. But, after a while, this began to bother us. Our schooled voices told us that *all* data should be recorded. Patiently we waited for Christian's work to take on the appearance of an assignment given out by a science teacher. Unfortunately, Christian had no preconceived notion as to how he should frame his research. His habitat study interested him greatly — but we worried that he wasn't learning the "scientific method"! This was when we began to interfere and ask him to measure his plot of land, to chart and graph his findings, and to take temperature readings on-site rather than at the bedroom window.

Now that the project was dead, David and I looked back over the sequence of events and began to understand our failings. What was wrong with allowing Christian to measure the air temperature at our bedroom window rather than at the site of his study? Nothing. It was Christian who had come up with the notion of taking temperature readings in the first place; in the process he learned to compare Fahrenheit and Celsius thermometer readings. What was wrong with allowing him to write down some of his data and not others? Nothing. Christian had worked with Donna on other projects and already knew how to make formal displays of his findings. What, then, would have been wrong with simply letting Christian conduct his habitat study as he saw fit? Nothing! In fact, he might have stuck with it longer and learned more had we kept out of his unschooled way of thinking.

Christian becomes a teenager

By the time Christian entered his teen years, we had become somewhat familiar with his natural rhythms of learning. For a few months he'd be immersed in learning about theater make-up or some other interest. Often, such interests would naturally and slowly fade from the horizon. At such times, Christian usually sank into a period of "do-nothingness." These periods of inactivity were often accompanied by parental fretting. If our worries got the best of us, we might nag him about finding something to do with himself. More frequently, though, we'd remind ourselves of all that Christian *was* doing: singing in choir, studying German, reading books, working on this or that volunteer project. Over time, we learned that these idle periods of his life were just as important as those periods when he was absorbed in some interesting project. He needed time to relax, to reflect on what he had learned, and to generate new energy to carry him in new directions.

As we thought about it, it seemed to us that Christian's need to laze about was a significant part of his development. We realized that even though his self-education didn't follow traditional academic time-lines, he still needed "study" breaks — but not necessarily the traditional summer, winter, and spring breaks. Christian's academic life, being entirely under his own control, never followed such a rigid routine; rather, he took breaks as *he* needed them. When we understood this, our only concern was that such periods of lethargy would not become too stressful for other family members.

But sometimes they did, and one such period became a turning point in Christian's early teen years. When he was fourteen, he had been complaining for quite some time about not knowing what to do with himself. If we offered suggestions, he would say, "But I don't feel like doing that," or, "You're my parents, you are responsible for educating me." As our frustration grew with these discussions, we'd simply remind Christian not to nag us with his complaints if he had no intention of following our suggestions. But one fateful Saturday afternoon, Christian started whining to me about being bored at just the wrong time! I lost my cool and sent him on his way. As he trudged off to his room, I went in search of David.

After David and I had commiserated with one another, we decided that we needed to take some decisive action. After an hour of talking together, we came up with a plan that, although scary for us to consider, seemed our only alternative. We called Christian to our room and outlined a set of choices he must consider: (1) he could enroll in public school; (2) he could let us purchase a curriculum that he would agree to follow; or (3) he could figure out something to do on his own. We were not sure what choice Christian would make. He had already been taking an advanced German course at the local high school, so he might decide in favor of going to school. After devoting thirteen years to homeschooling, we hoped he wouldn't make that choice. Christian's second option was almost as distasteful to us. Following the guidelines of a correspondence course would limit — for the first time — Christian's choices about what and how to learn. Christian knew, from talking to other "correspondence schooled" homeschoolers, that this might be a possibility. And, of course, he was personally familiar with his third option. We told Christian that whatever he chose to do, David and I were ready to support him. Christian was quite unhappy with our ultimatum but listened to us explain the details of each of the choices. He thought about it a bit, and then told us he'd try to figure out something to do with his time. He went off to his room to think. David and I felt bad for resorting to such manipulative means to get Christian to stop making our home life so disagreeable. While we waited, we called our friend, Sue, a fellow lifetime homeschooler, for support. Sue reminded us that she had also reached the end of her rope many times in the past fifteen years. With great understanding and sympathy, she assured us that hitting rock bottom was all part of normal homeschooling life.

As David and I said thanks and goodbye to Sue, there was a knock on the door. It was Christian. He quietly entered and handed me a scrap of paper on which he'd scribbled the words: "I want to learn all there is to know about ice fishing." As promised, we agreed without hesitation that this would be an interesting subject to pursue, and we made a date to take Christian to the library on Monday.

Ice fishing! Who would have thought! But, come Monday, Christian went to the library and rummaged the stacks. He found books galore on ice fishing, ice fishing equipment, bait needs, and prime fishing locations. He selected the books that interested him the most and checked out his limit. When he got home, he stacked them by his bed and began to immerse himself in the study of ice fishing. David and I were delighted that Christian had finally found something of interest to study and that he was once again enjoying every moment of the day.

A river runs through our house

As Christian got deeper and deeper into his study of ice fishing, I was relieved — and a bit anxious. I was relieved, of course, because he was no longer nagging me about what to do with himself. On the other hand, I found I was starting to worry about whether he should be spending so much time studying fishing. In these moments, I tried to remember how easy it had been for me to get in the way of his habitat study.

Why was I feeling this way again when confronted with one of my children's authentic learning ventures?

As I worked out the reasons for this, I saw that my discomfort arose because it didn't resemble anything like a school project. For the first week or two, Christian was doing appropriate "school work" because he was "studying" ice fishing books. Then Christian began to purchase ice-fishing equipment. As a well-trained schoolteacher, this made me uncomfortable. Fishing equipment wasn't "educational resources," was it?

Luckily, I spoke to David about my anxieties before saying anything to Christian. David, in his very clear-headed way, reminded me that Christian's current work was the essence of what we had been striving for ever since we'd taken up unschooling. Here he was, immersed in a study that fascinated him and that had significance in his own life. David's only concern was that the freeze on the lakes seemed to be taking its time this year. I took David's words to heart and kept out of Christian's hair.

Weeks of study turned into months, and eventually years, of study. Christian soon found a new direction: fly fishing. One of his books mentioned the use of flies rather than bait. The book illustrated the fly and described how to tie it. This fascinated Christian, so he purchased a few supplies and tried to tie an ice-fly. This led him to research more fly patterns. Before long, his research on fly patterns led him to the discovery of fly fishing. Soon he was reading about fly fishing and was tying flies five and six hours a day. Slowly, he developed his tying skills until he was able to tie flies nearly as well as a professional fly-tyer.

Christian had discovered fly fishing in the middle of winter and now he pined for spring. While he waited, he joined a fly-fishing club and began attending meetings. At those meetings, he met more experienced adult fly-tiers who admired his work, and even some fishing-shop owners who offered to sell his flies through their shops. At these meetings, and through his own reading and video viewing, he began to learn about "reading" rivers, "matching the hatch," and casting.

As spring and his birthday drew near, David and I decided to buy Christian a fly rod. By this time he'd been studying the art for six months, and had passed the fly fishing bug on to David! They wanted nothing more than to get out to a river and fish. We managed to find two good rods and reels on sale at a local sporting goods store. The morning we gave Christian his rod, he stared at it in disbelief and then, almost immediately, took it to the greenway behind our house and began experimenting with casting. Soon he was spending hours casting. As he got the rhythm of casting down, he began teaching David. When the season opened, both David and Christian went to a nearby trout stream as often as possible; and they enrolled in any casting clinics they could find. When David was unavailable to drive Christian to the trout streams, he took city buses, or got me to drive him to a small pond on the campus where he could fish for hours. There seemed to be no keeping him from streams and ponds.

Despite Christian's happy preoccupation, I still struggled with my worries about the educational value of studying fly fishing. I didn't mention my doubts to Christian but, as I'd done earlier, I discussed them with David instead. In order to reassure me, David read to me from some of Christian's trout fishing books — about the ancient origins of fly fishing, dating back to the time of Cleopatra and Caesar; about the simple life cycle of the mayfly and the complex life cycle of the caddis and stone flies; and about all of the Latin genus and species names of various flies that Christian had learned and used in discussions with David about entomology and ichthyology. David shared with me a second book, devoted to a discussion of stream and river ecology, and "reading" the water. He also suggested I watch a fishing video with Christian. The following afternoon, Christian and I watched a video that demonstrated the art of casting. This was physics: how the angle of the arm and wrist affects the momentum of the rod and line.

This was reassuring; now I could see that not only was fishing a study of biological sciences, it also included natural science, history, mathematics and foreign language. As I realized this, I understood that Christian had discovered, on his own, the deep interconnectedness of subject matter that I, as a schoolteacher, had been trained to think of only as isolated segments. His intuitive need to study fishing had brought him into the world as it really is: a natural blend of science, history, foreign language, art, reading, and so much more. Finally, it was apparent to me that his study of fishing, music, radio engineering, French, German, and many other interests, were part of the natural flow of his self-education, and were contributing to his well-rounded development as a young man.

Learning to let go

As parents and teachers, we had become critical of traditional educational practices. When we began our homeschooling venture we were confident that we'd be able to overcome all that we'd been trained to believe and simply begin unschooling without ever looking back. But that wasn't to be the case. It took quite a few failures before we discovered what it was that Christian needed from us. When we started to teach him how to write, we began with the same method that we'd been taught. When he wanted to do a habitat study, we tried to make it conform to what we knew about such projects when schooled children did them. As a result, Christian, like many schooled children, lost interest. After many such failures, we realized that our criticisms of the public school system could be applied to us as well! Finding our way as unschoolers was more difficult than we'd imagined it would be.

As Christian and Georgina each found new and fascinating things to learn about, David and I had to learn again and again how to surrender to our children's self-directedness. The fact that they were naturally quite different from each other helped us see that they needed to find their own individual path to a well-rounded education. As Christian and Georgina followed these different paths, we came to appreciate even more the difficulties all educators face — whether homeschool or public school — as they try to accommodate the differences among their students. Helping students learn not only the "basics," but also how to find their own individual paths, is a difficult art, that, for us, required the fortitude to leave classroom expectations behind and let our children lead the way to their own education.

·⚜ Chapter 7 ⚜·

How Will We Ever Conquer Math?

One day, when Christian was six, I told him he had just twenty minutes left to play, and that that wouldn't be very much time. He said, "That's more than ten minutes." "Yes," I agreed, "it's twice as much as ten minutes." "It's four fives," he rejoined. I asked him how he knew that. He responded, "Five plus five equals ten and five plus five equals ten and there are two tens in twenty, so there are four fives."

AT AGE FOUR, GEORGINA LOVED TO PLAY PARCHEESI. She had learned to count each of the dots on her die before moving her piece. After counting out one dot on one die, four on another die, and moving five spaces she said to me, "You can make five by four and one." Later she rolled a three and a two, counted them out and carefully moved her piece. "There are two ways to make five," she declared, "three and two, and four and one."

We struggle with mathematics

Reading was an activity that was a natural and normal part of our daily family life. But opportunities to integrate basic math skills into daily activity were not easy to find. David and I worried about how to help our children achieve mastery of these skills without making them dislike math, as so many children seemed to do.

My own childhood memories of math books and flash cards were mostly unpleasant. Full of algorithm drills, the books provided no context for the work we were expected to do. Story problems were at a minimum and activities involving creative problem-solving were almost non-existent. We children were simply instructed to churn out answer after answer to arithmetic problems. With few exceptions, math was a tedious task, which I hated and which often brought me to tears.

It was years later, in a college math course for prospective elementary school teachers, that I discovered that mathematics could be taught using games and manipulative materials. This made me see that math could be fun for children and offer them opportunities for exploration and discovery. For the first time in years, I remembered that when I was young, I had enjoyed solving math problems in my head, imaginatively making my pages of drills into story problems, learning tricks that helped me memorize tables, and, best of all, using math when I went to the store, or sewed, or cooked, or played various board and card games.

When I began teaching my visually-impaired students, I tried to bring my new enthusiasm for math to my students. To reinforce their arithmetic lessons with instruction in braille, I would take that opportunity to go beyond textbooks by using attribute blocks, peg boards, Unifix Cubes, balances, cards, and board games like *Monopoly* and *Life*. Such work clearly taught my students a great deal about math and excited their curiosity about numbers.

Numbers fascinate curious children

Both of our children's interest in numbers seemed to develop quite naturally between the ages of three and four. On long car rides, they made a game of counting higher and higher. By the time both children were five, they had discovered the rudimentary elements of addition and subtraction. David and I read the children "counting" books and gave them inexpensive math workbooks to play with. Of course we'd also introduced them to my favorite system for teaching about math: Cuisenaire rods. At toy stores and garage sales, we found games that used mathematical concepts. Cooking, building, sewing, violin lessons, educational TV shows, and trips to the bank and grocery store became natural opportunities for both children to learn, without much stress, about how to use numbers in their lives.

When our children were quite young, David and I were often amazed by the mathematical concepts they had so naturally absorbed. By the age of six or seven, they readily solved complex, real-life math problems in their heads, such as computing that the change from a $5.00 bill for a $1.53 purchase was $3.47, or dividing a deck of 36 cards into four even piles of nine each without using paper and pencil or trial-by-error. Clearly our children were developing mathematical reasoning skills, and yet, as in the case of Georgina's reading, when they couldn't come up with the answer to a simple question, such as "How much is 9+6?" we worried about the seeming inconsistencies in their abilities. Trusting that our children would someday know all of their addition, subtraction, multiplication and division, was not something we could easily do.

David and I continually discussed our concerns, and found a pattern. When they couldn't recite an answer to a basic math problem, we worried — and forgot that Christian or Georgina could mentally compute correct change. Reminded of their abilities, we realized that their real math abilities were more valuable than rote work. Such discoveries helped us trust in our children's natural abilities to work with numbers.

Christian struggles with math

Unfortunately, as our children got older, real life experiences that provided opportunities for converting percents to decimals or fractions, or averaging, or adding fractions, or the division of decimals, or other kinds of mathematical instruction were more difficult to come by. So, after much discussion, we finally decided to get some textbooks to help our children gain a solid understanding of basic mathematics.

When Christian was ten, he said he wanted to work with decimals and percents, and also to learn some geometry. Neither David nor I had the time to work out a sequentially progressive math program for him, so we turned to *Key Curriculum* materials, which had a series of "user friendly" workbooks covering fractions, decimals, percents, geometry and algebra. Christian looked over the workbooks and decided that he wanted to work with them. In the meantime, I retrieved some discarded textbooks that our school district was giving away. Using a combination of *Key Curriculum* workbooks and these "outdated" textbooks, Christian began to work to improve his math skills.

At this point, Christian's confidence in his ability to understand math was low. David and I did what we could to assure him that his mathematical reasoning skills were excellent, but this seemed to offer him no comfort. He understood that he had little interest in memorizing tables and algorithms, and concluded that he was a failure as a math student. Christian shed many tears over this. Although we tried to help him understand that his ability to reason — the most difficult part of becoming mathematically fluent — was excellent, and that we were sure he could memorize the details of mathematics if he would be patient with himself, we were never successful.

When the *Key Curriculum* materials arrived, Christian enthusiastically dove into the geometry workbook. He enjoyed working on the construction of geometric figures, and he spent hours at it. He became quite particular about his work. At one point, he felt that our five-and-dime compass was not suitable, and, taking some of his hard-earned paper route money, he went to the University bookstore to purchase a better compass. Needless to say, David and I were pleased to see that Christian was finding pleasure in his work.

When Christian completed the geometry books, he started in on the decimal and percent workbooks. Although he didn't want to, he felt he must. To help him, we purchased *Hands-On Equations*, a small curriculum packet designed to teach young children how to solve complex linear equations using dice and pawns. When Christian couldn't face decimals or percents, we'd get out *Hands-On Equations*. At first, things went smoothly, but soon he also lost interest in *Hands-On Equations*.

Later, when Christian turned twelve, his hopes of learning math revived when he participated in a teen discussion group at our annual homeschooling conference. There he heard many teens talking about Saxon Math materials, and felt they might be just what he needed. Our hopes were high. But again, after working with the Saxon books for a few months, Christian lost interest. We tried everything to help him, but nothing seemed to work. It was becoming evident that Christian's stress over math was getting in the way of his enjoyment of other things. Although David and I were confident that Christian could do well in math if he'd apply himself, there was no convincing him of this.

Christian finally gives up

In the fall of what would have been his freshman year in high school, Christian made one more gallant attempt to tackle math. He persuaded us to buy the Saxon *Algebra 1/2* textbook. David and I thought this would be appropriate since Christian's basic math skills seemed to be strong. When the book arrived, Christian spent a few weeks working with it. We thought that finally, Christian seemed to be making inroads into higher math. Unfortunately, one Monday morning, Christian didn't do as well as he would have liked on a section review test. This put him into another tailspin. He came to me in tears saying that he was simply a lousy student when it came to math.

It was heartbreaking for me to see Christian in such a state. David and I knew well that Christian was a wonderfully capable child, and yet all that he could see, at that moment, was that he was a failure. He hated feeling that way and began to talk about giving up on math altogether.

It scared him to broach such a subject with me, and yet he truly felt this was his only way out. He was in such conflict: on the one hand, he wanted to quit math; on the other hand, he knew that if he ever wanted to go to college he'd have to be able to do higher math. With patience, I expressed my confidence in his abilities to take on and learn math when the need was really present. I explained to him that at fourteen, with college at least four years away, there was no imminent call to learn higher math. I told him that when he needed to learn math for college or some other purpose, I was sure he'd learn what he needed to learn. As tears streamed down his cheeks, he decided that quitting the study of math might be in his best interest. With some difficulty, he set aside his books and applied himself wholeheartedly to other endeavors.

We accepted and even encouraged this decision because, by this time, we had seen that our children were capable of educating themselves at their own pace. We'd also read someplace that it only takes four months to learn all of high school math, and this helped us maintain our confidence in Christian's decision. In fourteen years, he'd taught us that he was capable of teaching himself anything once the motivation was there and we were sure, by this time, that for math, things would be no different. With only minor concerns, we allowed the math textbooks to be shelved, and rejoiced when Christian became his happy self once again.

Christian learns higher math

Christian didn't pick up a math book for the next three years. His life was filled with fly fishing, radio engineering, the study of language, and other activities — all of which entailed the real-life use of mathematical skills in one form or another. In the fall of 1995, Christian decided that he wanted to go to college and asked us to purchase the Saxon *Algebra I* and *Algebra II* materials. Once again, Christian's self-motivation was drawing him to tackle tasks that were part of his self-determined personal goal. This time he had a need to study. He began to work at his algebra two to three hours a day, 2 to 3 days a week. Within five months, Christian had worked his way through the first book and part way through the second, before taking his ACT exams. Although he didn't score as high in math as he might have, his overall score put him within the top ten percent of all college-bound graduating seniors — which pleased him no end! Now Christian would be able to attend college with such a good showing on the ACT. Here was another illustration of the virtues of self-directed learning — he had managed to do so well without having to suffer through three years of traditional mathematical study at the expense of studying things that truly motivated him.

Georgina learns math her own way

David and I realized, early on, that Georgina, like Christian, had excellent mathematical reasoning ability, but disliked the rote work necessary to become a good mathematician. In an attempt to maintain Georgina's mathematical self-confidence, we decided to keep textbooks out of her life for as long as possible. Georgina greatly enjoyed playing commercial and homemade math games, although some of them were little more than glorified drill activities. These helped teach her algorithms for addition, subtraction, multiplication and division.

As in reading, Georgina required a slow-paced, individualized approach to learning basic math skills. For the most part, we were patient; but, as with her reading, when Georgina wasn't doing math for long periods of time, we interfered and required that she spend some time working with us on math skills. This, predictably, generated tension between us. Georgina complained that while we'd given her permission to work on math at her own pace, our word wasn't true. We acknowledged to her that we had agreed that she need not keep up with her schooled peers, and yet we had concerns. We tried to explain to her that, unlike reading, learning mathematical algorithms was not something that was naturally a part of our daily lives. Georgina's need for imaginative play, an active social life, and large doses of physical exercise, didn't present many opportunities to study arithmetic. As we recognized this, we talked to Georgina about our concerns and devised, with her help, plans for maintaining some sort of regular study of math.

Over time these conflicts concerning math between Georgina and us became quite unmanageable. The more freedom we gave Georgina to study at her own pace, the more we realized that she wasn't studying. We tried hard to explain to her that she was doing poorly simply because she was so sporadic in her studies. Together we tried to devise various methods to remedy the situation, but still nothing seemed to work.

Georgina finds her own reason to study math

When Georgina was thirteen she began thinking about going to high school. To help her, we began to meet regularly with her to help map out an easy transition into high school. As these meetings progressed, Georgina began to set very high standards for her study of math. By year's end, Georgina proudly announced that she'd finished the *Math 76* book and was ready to take a placement test to determine how to continue her study of math.

When Georgina had settled herself into a regular routine of studying math, she began to learn interesting things about herself. Unlike Christian, for her, math became easier with regular work. As she discovered this, she also developed an interest in going to college as an eighteen-year-old. At this time, she was observing Christian working his way through math books at breakneck pace in order to be prepared for the ACT, and she knew this wasn't the way she wanted to do things. As she said to me at the time, "I can't study the way Christian does. I'll have to work at math for the next two years."

Now, Georgina had come full circle, from dreading our reminders to keep at her math studies, to understanding that for her, the best method of study was to keep plugging away at it. When Georgina completed her placement test and scored well enough to begin *Algebra I*, David and I knew that her sense of pride in a task well-done was well-deserved. We never imagined that Georgina would set her goals on studying higher math, much less entering college in four years! She seemed to have discovered, through her work with math, that she was as capable as we'd always told her she was.

Letting go of our fears

It took David and me years to learn that it is best to surrender our traditional notions about education to the individual needs of our children. We shudder to think that we might have killed any interest Christian might have had in attending college simply because we force-fed him math at a time when he so desperately wanted to be done with it. Likewise, Georgina might never have discovered her mathematical talents had we insisted she begin using textbooks when Christian did, or that she keep "on grade level" with her schooled peers. In finally learning to follow the course our children set out for us, we maintained our ultimate goal in the homeschooling process. Christian and Georgina's overall curiosity and interest in learning stayed alive and even grew. Their initial lack of confidence as math students has not overshadowed their overall confidence in themselves, and thus they readily tackle many new and challenging explorations each day.

·≋ Chapter 8 ≋·

Georgina Learns To Read

I believe that we learn best when we, not others, are deciding what we are going to try to learn. — *John Holt,* What Do I Do Monday?

WHEN SHE WAS EIGHT, our high-spirited and energetic daughter, Georgina, broke her leg and faced a long convalescence. With her full-length cast and crutches she became easily frustrated, ornery and restless. To help ease her unhappiness, I read more often to her. Months later, Georgina wrote a report entitled: "All About Chimps"

My mom started reading books to me about ladies studying apes. They studied apes all their life. One of these women was Jane Goodall. Jane studied chimps. While Jane studied chimps she was in Africa. She went to Africa with her mother. Her mother stayed in the jungle camp and cooked meals. Jane found a group of chimps. She climbed the nearest tree to study them. She did this for many months

Chimps live in the rain forests of Africa. Africa is in the southern hemisphere. The southern hemisphere gets hotter than the northern hemisphere. Chimps live in groups of 20 to 25. There are usually three chimps in a family. There is a mother, a father and baby. There is usually one male in a group of chimps. That male chimp is the leader of the group. He is the only one who is allowed to mate. The other males are too young to mate.

Chimps always care for each other. If a chimp gets sick other chimps will take care of it. Mother chimps groom baby chimps after they play. Mothers pick dirt and bugs off the baby chimps. They eat the bugs. In a chimp group, there are quite a few juveniles. They are not babies or grownups. The juveniles are not old enough to take care of themselves. They play a lot. Chimps spend most of their time looking for food. They look for fruit and leaves. If they can't find a lot of that then they hunt. Chimps are the only apes who hunt.

As Christian and Georgina followed their own interests to create unorthodox learning adventures, we began to get glimpses of what seemed to be so right about the unschooling process. Studying make-up design had taught Christian the importance of considering the infinite detail of color and form, and creating flies to lure a trout — an art he studied intensely for four years — is based on just such attention to detail. By working to perfect her swim strokes, Georgina learned the importance of staying with a repetitive process even if it was boring; today, as she works on monologues and scripts, she understands that although the work may be tedious, it is essential to creating believable characters.

As our children lived and learned, they unintentionally demonstrated the connection between one learning experience and the next. Over time, David and I learned to look for the valuable connections between all the things our children did. Our experiences confirmed what John Holt had written in *What Do I Do Monday?*

> I believe that we learn best when we, not others, are deciding what we are going to try to learn, and when, and how, and for what reasons or purposes; when we, not others, are in the end choosing the people, materials, and experiences from which and with which we will be learning; when we, not others, are judging how easily or quickly or well we are learning, and when we have learned enough; and above all when we feel the wholeness and openness of the world around us, and our own freedom, power and competence in it.

Holt's words had been among many that had led us to make our initial venture into unschooling. Now, we were beginning to recognize the interconnections between music, foreign language and creative expression; and between music, juggling and fly casting. We found comfort knowing that Christian and Georgina were creating, for themselves, well-connected and meaningful lives.

However, as our children spread their wings to take on such challenging learning ventures, David and I had to confront our reluctance to let them take charge when it came to their learning reading and math on their own. This didn't become apparent to us until our children challenged our assumptions about such matters.

Will she ever read?

When Georgina was five and Christian was nine, we were officially homeschooling two children. Christian had learned to read with ease, but Georgina seemed to have no interest in becoming the same kind of fluent reader. Before we registered Georgina as a homeschooler, we had been quite comfortable letting her discover reading in her own time and manner. But now that she was registered with the Department of Public Instruction, suddenly we started worrying about her limited sight vocabulary, her lack of any more than a cursory sense of letter sounds, and her seeming disinterest in improving either of these skills. Although she'd read her first words at an earlier age than Christian, and she "wrote" (i.e., dictated, or wrote in her own phonetic language) wonderfully creative stories at an earlier age than Christian, all we could see was that Georgina wasn't learning to read as we'd expected she would — that is, as we'd been trained to expect all children would.

As David and I discussed our concerns, we considered all we knew about Georgina. As an infant, she crawled and stood unaided at an earlier age than Christian had; yet she walked at a later age than he had. But, unlike Christian, once Georgina began to walk, she ran! As a baby learning to talk, she followed a similar pattern, beginning to talk at a later age than Christian did. But once she began to talk, she spoke fluently and, like her brother, used whole complex sentences with ease. Was this well-established learning pattern going to work with reading as well?

When Georgina was an infant, we never doubted that she would one day walk and talk. As parents of a preschooler, there were no social pressures on us regarding appropriate time-lines for her to learn these skills. Yet, we knew all too well the main public perceptions about homeschooling. The positive one was that homeschooling was the perfect solution to all the problems of public schooling. The negative message was that homeschooling would cause academic retardation and social ineptitude. Having lived the life of homeschoolers for nine years, we knew that neither of these statements was true — but still we worried. We didn't want to be thought responsible for academically retarding our children and raising them as social misfits, and we felt the pressure to create the perfect educational environment. As the product of schools, we'd been trained to believe that children should begin reading by age six. Given Georgina's current reading skills, we didn't see her fitting that mold any time soon.

We had been taught that when children don't keep up basic skills, they risk never being able to master those skills. Could it be that we were still skeptical of John Holt's unschooling approach to learning? Years of traditional schooling, teacher training, and teaching had deeply affected both of us. Our children were fearless as they dabbled in reading, or experimented with music or explored our community. We, on the other hand, feared they wouldn't accumulate appropriate knowledge or skills to enable them to compete and get ahead in the world. Gripped by such fears, we once again had to consider whether to turn to the schools for help, or continue to homeschool.

Happily, our successes with Christian had given us a taste of the miracles that unschooling could yield. Sending Georgina to school seemed hypocritical to us. She was, after all, flourishing in many arenas. She was very comfortable with people of all ages, she enjoyed learning new things and, most important, she was an enthusiastically energetic and happy child. As we considered Georgina's happiness and well-being, we realized we had to maintain our unschooled life style, if at all possible. It was of particular importance to do so when our beliefs about learning got in the way of her intuitive sense of how best to learn. She had, after all, succeeded in learning much on her own. We had a lot to lose and nothing to gain if we meddled. Thank heaven, Georgina was a spirited child! She gave us little option but to trust in her inner drive to learn.

As David and I did some soul-searching on how we might help Georgina learn to read, I reflected on all that I knew about teaching reading. As a teacher who had traveled from school to school, I had considerable experience with many different methodologies. Each school and each school district that I had worked in taught reading differently, using phonetic alphabets, or phonics, or "look and say," or "whole language" approaches to teaching reading. From working with these different methodologies, I knew the pros and cons of each.

The phonetic alphabet approach requires the use of special reading material, introducing children to an alphabet in which one phonetic symbol represents each different sound in our language. By the time children who have been taught to read using this method reach the age of six or seven, their teachers slowly convert them to reading "Standard English." I remembered one of my first students asking me, "Alison, when will you begin to teach me to do real reading?" Hadn't I been teaching Danny to read since becoming his vision teacher? What did he think I was teaching him when we worked on braille code together? But Danny's classmates were learning to read from books written with a phonetic alphabet, and, since braille code has no equivalent, I had been brailling his pre-primers and readers in standard English from the start. When I explained to him that he'd always been doing "real" reading and that he was already way ahead of his friends, his expression changed from worry to calm and we resumed our lesson. Likewise, it seemed to us that it made no sense to teach Georgina to read an alphabet she'd never find in books. Besides, the cost of purchasing such books was out of the question.

Next, I considered phonics. When I was a child, my teachers had used phonics as part of their reading programs, and as a teacher, I'd worked with other teachers who did the same. But using phonics required lots of drill work and memorization, and this was a considerable drawback as far as Georgina was concerned. Making her do drill work and memorize rules would surely kill what little interest in reading she had. On the other hand, to a beginning reader, it would be useful to know that particular combinations of letters generally yielded particular sounds. Georgina, not being the type of child who could sit still for drill work or memorizing, could perhaps benefit from having us use phonics as a reinforcement for skills that she might already have.

The third method I considered was the familiar "look and say" approach. This method is based on memorization. Word lists and word families (sat, cat, rat, hat) are used to create reading material that has a controlled vocabulary. I'd worked extensively with this method and felt that in some cases it was more confusing than helpful to children. Sentences like, "The fox on the box had the pox," don't lend themselves to helping children learn to read. Stories based on such limited vocabularies give children nothing to make meaningful, real life sense of. Instead, children must pay more attention to decoding skills, whereas I knew that fluency as a reader came from being able to use the context of the reading material to help decipher words and meaning. Again, knowing Georgina, I was pretty sure that she wouldn't want to sacrifice meaningful reading for memorization of words and word lists. I might have luck using some of the "look and say" approach, but I knew we couldn't bank on teaching her to read if we relied on it solely.

I asked myself whether or not Georgina was asking us to "teach" her to read. Clearly she wasn't. Georgina was more interested in being read to than learning to read. We had always provided an assortment of opportunities for Georgina to experience reading. She loved being read to, and she liked books on tape and record, and educational TV shows in which authors read their stories. She was drawn to any story that was well-read or dramatized. These activities seemed to draw her into a world rich in imaginative play. She would spend hours working to perfect her oral expression and develop different character voices. She could recite entire chapters from Beverly Cleary's Ramona Quimby books. As she recited, she would imitate the different characters' voices as she'd heard the actress who read the stories do. This dramatic activity did not represent an invitation for us to teach Georgina to read. Rather, she seemed to be asking us to continue to read to her and provide her with opportunities to hear stories being read aloud.

Georgina's lack of interest in becoming a reader was her parents' problem, not hers. She had no difficulty with the fact that she was six and uninterested in gaining any more reading knowledge than she already had. At this time, I began thinking about what schools termed the "whole language" approach to reading. This method relies on ordinary books that one might find in libraries, bookstores, or on the living room shelf. Reading material can come from books, magazines, comics or any other printed source that interests the budding reader. The "whole language" approach to teaching reading is highly individualized. Not only are children allowed to select their own reading materials, they are also encouraged to write their own if they find nothing of interest! Such an approach to reading doesn't single out reading as an individual subject to be taught but rather allows reading to be an integral part of the school day. It simply requires that children be free to explore reading in ways that suit their individual needs and interests. I'd never thought of dramatizing stories as part of such a process, but why not? Georgina was certainly being exposed to reading. In fact, she was so well-exposed that she was memorizing major portions of her favorite books. Of all that I knew about teaching reading, the "whole language" method had always seemed to be the most sensible approach of all. Now it seemed to be the most sensible approach to use with our homeschooled daughter as well.

Georgina becomes a reader — in her own way

My experiences as a special education teacher had been instrumental in helping us decide to homeschool our own children. I'd seen Germain and many other students lose interest in their learning. Children learned to read in classrooms according to the school district's overall time-line for teaching reading. There was no such thing as grouping together children who were eager to learn to read, and allowing other children to explore different avenues of learning. I'd seen many children who had come to school excited to learn lose interest because they were forced to learn according to someone else's lesson plans. Many of these children came to hate reading.

Georgina seemed to be saying that she would learn to read in her own good time. At age three, she had read her first words; by four, she increased her reading vocabulary by a few more words and even more by age five; yet she was not consuming books as Christian had. By age six, we saw more improvement in her reading ability, but still no interest in sitting down with piles of books just for the joy of reading. Instead, Georgina seemed to want to listen to us reading to her and then replay the fantasies in the stories she heard. We were coming to understand that our sole job as parents was to keep Georgina's joy of reading alive for that time in the future when she'd be ready to master the skill. Never mind decoding skills, word recognition quizzes and comprehension tests!

This wasn't always easy to do, however. In our weaker moments, when Georgina seemed to have gone for quite some time without reading anything at all, we'd ask her to spend specified time reading. Content was not an issue, nor was the ability level of the material; we simply wanted her to read. At other times, when she was reading in her typically sporadic manner, we didn't make an issue of it. When she read, we were content. When she didn't, we worried and asked her to read. When we were at the library, while she selected books for me to read to her, I selected books she might be able to read on her own. In the afternoons and evenings, we played board games that required reading. We had an old encyclopedia set that she enjoyed browsing through and putting book marks in (always at articles about a favorite animal).

By the time Georgina was seven, we recognized that when she read aloud such things as: "To ensure the survival of the caribou, man must not interfere in their seasonal migrations across the tundra" (from *Wildlife Adventure*, a Ravensburger board game); or, "You and your mate compose a beautiful whale song. Go forward six spaces. All other whales go forward two. ...Whale Fact: Songs sung by humpbacks seem to be different every year" (from *The Whale Game*, a Wildlife Games, Inc., board game) — she really *was* reading. It wasn't reading of the sort that we had been trained to think of as "real" reading, but she was indeed reading. Once we understood this, our worries ceased to be so burdensome. The payoff for allowing Georgina to learn to read in her own time was very rewarding. From listening to taped books for hours, not only did Georgina learn to read aloud with real expression and rhythm, she enjoyed reading that neither of us would have expected she might.

When Georgina was ten, a local radio station asked her and David to read from a book of poetry written in two-part verse, *Joyful Noise: Poems for Two Voices* by Paul Fleischman. The night of the broadcast, I listened, with my breath held, while David and Georgina performed, almost flawlessly, the most difficult reading I'd ever imagined: two-part choral reading! It was like listening to two-part harmony, but instead of a song, it was poetry being performed. And later, as she became a budding actress, I'd hear Georgina in her bedroom, reading aloud again and again memorizing lines that she would be performing for her audiences. How unnecessary it now seemed to have worried about whether or not she was "on track" as a reader when she was six. As a teenager, she could read with the best of them, and her oral expression — the part of reading she was most drawn to as a six-year-old — was getting her parts in plays to boot!

⟐ Chapter 9 ⟐

Revisiting School

"Billy, are you stupid?" a loud booming voice shouted. The chatter of children's voices stopped. Again, from down the hallway came another loud and threatening inquiry, "Billy, I asked you, are you stupid?"

As I walked quickly down the hall, I heard Billy say, "No," his voice trembling. "Well, only stupid kids try to leave the building using this door, so you must be stupid!"

I couldn't believe my ears: it was the elementary school principal, my fellow educator. How could any adult, especially one in the position of educating children, so humiliate a child? Was this what discipline in schools was coming to? Children who made mistakes deserved, above anything else, respectful correction from those adults who are educators and caregivers. What was happening in our schools anyway? Were things as bad as the media were saying they were?

— Notes from my teaching journal, 1990

As our family grew, we decided I needed to find occasional work to supplement our income. Tutoring visually-impaired students would provide me with job flexibility and enough income to help us get by. Such work would also keep me in touch with what schools were doing. Occasionally, I also accepted work as a substitute teacher. My experiences as both tutor and substitute played a significant part in helping us become more confident in ourselves as unschooling parents, and gave me insights into the problems of our current educational system.

Should I teach full-time?

Tutoring gave me the flexible hours I wanted, but within a few years, David and I began to think that if I selectively accepted substitute teaching jobs, our financial needs would be better met. It wasn't long before

I was interviewed for a full-time substitute teaching position in a preschool.

By the end of the interview, however, I had sincere doubts that I should take the job. First, our children would need child care. Christian could attend a full-day learning center located in a teacher's home; Georgina would have to attend day-care or be taken care of by friends. Christian asked, "What happens when the teacher makes me do something that bores me? Do I have to do it?" David and I were quick to see how difficult it would be to insist that Christian follow a teacher's lesson plans when our decision to homeschool was based on allowing *him* to decide what was important to study. And what about Georgina? How would she feel being shuffled from one day-care home to the next? If she didn't want to play at a friend's house, what then? Being bored wasn't the issue — we had nothing against their being bored on their *own* terms, just as we had nothing against play on their *own* terms — it was just that we had come to wholeheartedly believe in the value of their self-motivation to educate themselves.

The second source of doubt that arose as a result of my interview was more philosophical. Over the years, I'd come to question the role of structured teaching for young children. Now, faced with structured preschool education, I was more uncomfortable than ever. Could I put my concerns aside and look the other way just for the sake of earning a few extra dollars?

After talking it over with David, I knew that such work couldn't be integrated into our family routine without great emotional cost and compromise of my principles. I was already losing sleep just thinking about it. What would happen if I went against my feelings and took this job? Where would I be at the end of six weeks? How would our children fare? The sense that there wasn't a thing to gain and everything to lose became clearer the more I mulled it over. When, a week after my interview, I was offered the job, I informed them I had decided to decline it.

Living life by the bell at home

Gradually, I slowly picked up tutoring jobs. While these jobs helped us meet the ever-increasing costs of raising a family, they interrupted our family routines. Often the new jobs were sandwiched into the study hall periods of my clients. This meant that the natural rhythms of our family life, which we'd worked so hard to create, were constantly being interrupted — by school bells! While Georgina told me about her work at the pet store or at the "Y", I would nervously watch the clock: "You'll have to tell me the rest later, honey, I've got to go to school now." More than once I had to cut short Christian's reference searches at the public library so I could get him home before heading off for a tutorial lesson with one of my students.

It was difficult for me to come to terms with these demands on my time and my beliefs. I knew my students benefited from their time with me and our family benefited from the extra income. But how could I support a system that seemed so dysfunctional? And was it fair to deprive my own children of the time and support I wanted to give them? Was it a greater good to help other children in the schools or to help mine at home? I didn't want to help maintain an education system I disapproved of, yet I didn't want to abandon the great kids I was helping. There were no easy answers.

And, of course, we had to consider our finances, especially as our children might someday want to attend college. To help finance such a venture, it was likely that I'd have to return to teaching full time at some point, but every time we discussed this, I became upset. My tutoring was making it clear, with every class period I spent in the schools, that working under such conditions was very difficult for me. It was becoming almost impossible to imagine myself teaching on a full-time basis.

However, we tried not to let such conversations dominate our thoughts. Instead, we continued to immerse ourselves in the lives of our children. More and more, we learned to trust them to follow their instincts. As my tutoring in the schools reminded us, a day of self-initiated library browsing was a far more productive use of our children's time than that typical 32 minutes of library time at the same time on the same day they would have received in school.

Exploring Egypt

When Georgina was eight and Christian twelve, I was offered another long-term substitute teaching position. At this juncture in our lives, David had job flexibility that would allow him to cover much of the time that I would be at work, and there were friendships and classes which both children wanted to explore when neither of us could be home. And, since I still had nagging concerns about the advantages and disadvantages of traditional education and unschooling, I felt that the opportunity for me to "work inside the system" might help me address those concerns with more clarity.

Some of my concerns were addressed sooner than expected. Two months before I began the job, Georgina had become fascinated with ancient Egyptian culture. This was something she had become interested in on one of our trips to the library. After bringing home a pile of books — such as *The Pyramids* by John Weeks, *Ancient Egypt* by George Hart, and *Mummies Made in Egypt* by Aliki — she began a slow but thoroughly enjoyable study of ancient Egyptian culture. This included reading — or having us read to her — from her selection of library books; playing a board game called "Pyramids and Mummies"; watching videos that took the viewer inside many of the ancient pyramids; writing with hieroglyphics; building a scale model of an Egyptian city; and daydreaming about life during the times of the great Pharaohs. On some days, Georgina and I would sit on the kitchen floor together and work on her scale model. On other days, we'd cuddle up on the couch to browse through the many picture books of Egypt that she'd checked out from the library. On still other days, Egypt wasn't a part of her daily activity. Her study of Egypt had a natural rhythm to it and all of us thoroughly enjoyed learning about it with her.

Then, on the first Monday in November when I started my new job, I was pleasantly surprised to find that I'd been assigned to team-teach in a sixth grade classroom where Egypt was the topic of study. How exciting! On that first day, my teaching peer led a review of last week's lesson for which I was to lead the small-group activities afterwards. But, to my dismay, I realized this study of Egypt was going to be nothing like the happy, absorbed hours that Georgina spent studying Egypt. It soon became clear that for these children, "Egypt" was a topic that was only to be discussed between 10:30 and 11:20 on Monday and Thursday; "Egypt" meant memorizing terms like "obelisk," "pyramid" and "mummy" for an upcoming multiple-choice test; and "Egypt" was also something that was going to be forgotten when the class moved on to "Greece" two weeks hence. As I listened to these children review their facts, I realized that no matter how interesting my plans for small-group activities might be, these children were limited by a school curriculum that said I must provide the lesson that they must absorb, whether or not they (or I) found it interesting.

Georgina's experience of Egypt was so much different, so much more alive. She talked about Egypt at breakfast, lunch, and dinner, and sometimes fell asleep listening to us read from her favorite books on Egypt. There were no tests or worksheets at the "end" of her study; indeed, there was no "end" to her study at all: she had a lifetime to complete it. My sixth graders, on the other hand, didn't have such a personal connection with their subject and they might never experience such joys, given the constraints put on them by the demands of curriculum, tests and worksheets.

Come Thursday, we had our second social studies class on Egypt. The teacher called the class to order.

"Please get out your books and the worksheets that you were to do for homework."

"Aw!" — a collective groan reverberated through the room as the children rummaged in their desks for books, paper and pencils. Corrections began.

"Number one. Who can identify the picture that is drawn in number one? Mary?"

"Yes, it's an obelisk."

"Good. Number two. 'Ra' was the god of what? Who can tell me what 'Ra' was the god of? Yes, Pete?"

My heart sank. I wondered how such an interesting subject could be made so deadly dull. Wasn't there something I could do in my small-group activities that would help bring Egypt to life for these children? Maybe I could read to them some of the literature Georgina had discovered. Better yet, why not let the children read whatever they wanted about Egypt. What about movies or field trips? Georgina had come up with the idea of building a scale model of an Egyptian city; maybe these kids would like some sort of hands-on activity like that.

During the next two weeks, I tried to implement my ideas. I gave the children opportunities to explore literature, create projects, and view movies and filmstrips. But I never sensed that such activities generated the same kind of love for the subject as it had for Georgina. Yes, what they were doing was fun, but these children were only skimming the surface of the learning experience. The time they had to study Egypt had a definite beginning and end, which prevented all of us — students and teachers — from becoming immersed in our work. When I realized this, all of my concerns that we might be harming our children by not following traditional curriculum content seemed unfounded.

Exploring math

A year later, I was offered another part-time substitute teaching job at a different school, working with visually impaired students. Part of my work was to teach two different levels of math to two different students — at the same time! Although I had never tried to do such a thing, I believed I'd be able to work out some sort of meaningful lessons for my students. After studying the materials that the children were working with and reviewing the teacher's notes about their strengths and weaknesses, I felt reasonably well-prepared.

My first week with Liz and Alex gave me a sense of my students' capabilities. Their skills were very different. Whereas Liz could solve almost any arithmetic problem that was put into braille for her, Alex's strength lay in his ability to mentally work out answers to complex story problems. Liz froze when I asked her to solve "word problems"; Alex froze when I asked him to solve problems that had only numbers. Both children felt inept because of their different "weaknesses."

By week's end, I had decided that moving back and forth between the children during our short class period was an inefficient use of my time. It also prevented both children from understanding the strengths that they *did* possess. Soon I began having the children work together, believing that, by helping each other, they would gain confidence in their own abilities. Although a bit uncertain about this arrangement, both children agreed to give it a try.

With the textbooks as my guide, we began to work together to solve arithmetic and story problems. I made a point of spending time on both types of problems so that neither child would feel inadequate. Alex helped Liz figure out story problems, while Liz helped Alex master arithmetic algorithms. As Alex put words to arithmetic problems so that Liz might understand how to solve them, his confidence in his own abilities grew. Likewise, Liz began to think of herself as capable at mathematics, as Alex, under her guidance, became more proficient. Both children benefited from working together and, quite frequently, we lost track of time and worked past the 48-minute class period.

As I worked with Alex and Liz over the next three months, I realized that my experience as a homeschooling parent had benefited these children. The flexibility that Christian and Georgina demanded had forced me to find new and interesting ways to facilitate their learning. As Liz and Alex's teacher, I'd been able to draw on this experience. By working out this method, I realized that schooled instruction need not necessarily hamper children's enthusiasm for learning. Strengths *and* weaknesses, different in each child, brought to work together, could create new understandings of how to promote individual learning.

Good ideas gone bad

However, my work with Alex and Liz was not always so rewarding. In more traditional teaching settings, my opportunities to facilitate such meaningful learning opportunities were hampered. Sometimes the structure of traditional schooling simply got in the way, despite the best efforts of my fellow teachers to use innovative and individualized instructional methods.

A startling example of this occurred when I began helping Alex and Liz with their reading. Their teachers team-taught their classes, using innovative methods to motivate their students, particularly in reading. Mrs. Jakowski used an individualized approach, letting each child read from self-selected material. She met with each child at least twice a week to discuss the reading each was doing. The children seemed to enjoy this individualized attention and gained much confidence in themselves as readers.

Unfortunately there was a down side: to give such individualized instruction, Mrs. Jakowski relied on her other students to either be reading or working on unrelated exercises — a weekly "packet" of assorted "word searches," or mathematical or scientific puzzles, or short group activities, or creative writing exercises. To me, these exercises were a pleasant change from the run-of-the-mill worksheets I was familiar with — but poor Alex hated them! To him, the "busy work" was extremely fatiguing. Because he had minimal useful vision, such "extra" (and unnecessary) work put a strain on his eyes. In order to help ease this strain, Alex and I worked together.

One Friday, Alex was working on one of the extra assignments, a particularly difficult math code. After spending a frustrating morning trying to help him with it, I noted in my teaching journal:

> I've just spent a whole morning working on a math sheet with Alex. We worked out a problem-solving tactic, to cut down on any unnecessary work. Once we outlined this plan of attack, we got down to work on the problem itself, but after an hour-and-a-half, we hadn't cracked the code.
>
> At break time, I asked Alex to check with friends to see if they had solved the problem, but none of them had come up with an answer, either. In fact, no one in the class could solve the problem. I decided to check in with Mrs. Jakowski, hoping that she would give me the answer to the problem so that I could get Alex headed in the right direction.
>
> Mrs. Jakowski told me she didn't know the answer to the problem nor did she have any intention of finding it! I asked her if she would be going

over the work with the rest of the class; she said she hadn't planned to. I then asked her if Alex could put the math problem aside.

"Alex, have you done your independent reading form?"

"Yes." She read it over. "Okay, you don't need to finish the math sheet."

Stunned, I asked Mrs. Jakowski where she'd like me to put Alex's work. He had 10 pages of figuring and I wanted her to see the work he had put into it. She told me "not to bother." I told her that I wanted to be sure Alex wouldn't be marked down for trying, but being unable to solve the problem.

"Oh, no, I don't grade weekly packets at all," she replied.

Here I sit, dumbfounded by the experience I've just gone through! Alex is expected to spend hours and hours of physically fatiguing work that has no bearing on his overall grades. It doesn't seem fair at all.

And yet, what was the alternative? Should I have advocated for group reading instruction, to eliminate so much pointless busy work? No, children need all the individualized attention they can get. That Mrs. Jakowski was providing these children with any opportunity for such instruction was wonderful. The problem is that if it happens at all, individualized instruction has to fit within the larger structure of the traditional school day. In this case, Mrs. Jakowski had opted for maintaining individualized instruction and used busy work to facilitate that instruction. In the best of all possible worlds, individualized instruction should be offered to each student as others work on projects that hold *real interest* for them. This, of course, was the essence of the homeschooling alternative, which can provide children the opportunity to learn in their own ways without the need for busy work. For now, though, I could only hope that Mrs. Jakowski and good teachers like her would continue to provide as much individualized instruction to children as they could.

Discipline: whose problem is it?

Students' complaints about school — a waste of time, too much busy work, boredom, dull subjects, unmotivated teachers — are pretty much the same complaints that I and my schoolmates voiced a generation ago. But are these complaints the cause of the increase in disciplinary problems that teachers face nowadays?

Not entirely. Since 1975, when I began teaching, I have seen many changes within the educational system — not all of them good. To me, the worst of those changes has been the increasing number of children labeled "learning disabled" and/or "emotionally disturbed." I believe that, in most instances, the label "disabled" signifies nothing more than a child who learns differently or is more expressive than his or her peers. In another setting, say homeschooling, such a child would likely be considered "normal." In addition, many of the teachers who work in these highly specialized and stressful situations come to their work ill-prepared to deal with discipline problems. As a result, many of the children in these "disability" programs are being mistreated by the very persons who are supposed to be the ones best able to help them learn! In my more recent tenure of work, it wasn't uncommon for me to be witness to examples of this problem, such as the following entry from my teaching journal:

> This afternoon, while I was working on my tutorial notes, I was distracted by a teacher rushing from her classroom to the school's main office. A moment later, the teacher rushed back, followed by the principal storming across the hall. I heard the principal yell, at the top of his lungs, "Go on, Ian. Are you going to pick up that chair and throw it at me, Ian? If you do, you'll be suspended!" Suddenly, my heart was racing. As the principal continued yelling, I could only imagine how that little boy must be feeling — like a caged and threatened animal. Would he try to protect himself from this apparently crazed adult, and strike out in self-defense?

After the yelling died down and the hallway full of curious onlookers cleared, and some kind of order was restored, I began to reflect on the situation I'd just witnessed. Who was more emotionally disturbed, the defiant student or the raging principal? Many afternoons, I had watched Ian playing happily on the playground with his peers. If he was truly emotionally disturbed, was the principal's display of temper an appropriate means of helping Ian center himself? Wouldn't levelheaded patience, nurturing and understanding have been a more appropriate approach to helping Ian calm down?

Such a display of hostility by adults in authority was nothing new to me. But it seemed to me that I'd seen more of such behavior in the schools in the past ten years. Why was there an increase in the verbal, and sometimes physical, abuse of children? Could it be the increasing inability of schools to deal with the individual needs of students? And the inadequacy of labeling such students "learning disabled?" And yet, I was reluctant to step into those situations and defend a child like Billy, who'd been humiliated for using the wrong door, or Ian, whose safety seemed to be threatened, against such rude and threatening adults. I felt powerless to intercede in a system that had created an "us against them" mentality. These were very troubling issues, indeed.

Schooling and homeschooling: some final thoughts

This book is a sampling of the experiences I've had as both a public school educator and a homeschooling parent. Much of what I've seen in the schools is bad: the humiliation of children by adults, boring lessons, bored students, unmotivated teachers, larger numbers of children being unnecessarily labeled "learning disabled," and poor treatment of our most needy students. Not all of what I've seen is bad, however: some teachers are attempting to individualize instruction; small-group work and hands-on activities are increasing; and more classrooms allow free movement between work stations.

My return to tutorial and substitute work did bolster our commitment to homeschooling. It clarified for us that our family's departure from traditional schooling was something we valued above all else. Finding satisfaction with our choice to homeschool was a freeing experience — and yet it did not make my work in the schools any easier. I know these are institutions to which I would not send my children, and yet I cannot imagine abandoning the children I help there. My satisfaction in helping these kids is too important to allow my dissatisfaction with the institution of school to get in the way.

I know schools will be with us for many generations to come. As bad as I've found them to be, I have to believe that they will improve. And I've come to believe that schools can learn a lot from homeschooling families like ours. Homeschooling families, across the country and around the world, have learned much about how to make education meaningful and interesting, and what we have learned in our living rooms can be of use to educators who are interested in reforming schools.

One of the great failures of our present-day educational system is that it is not individualized, nor does it take into account that everyone, students and teachers alike, has strengths to share with one another which will, in turn, broaden the capacities of our entire learning community. When Mrs. Jakowski lets her students individually select what they want to read, she is becoming a part of the educational reform movement. When Liz and Alex help one another learn math, they too are helping reform our educational system. This kind of helpful cooperation — teachers cooperating with students, students working with one another — must be the direction educational reform takes.

Homeschooling parents have learned much about this cooperative model of instruction. As our children have developed interests that go beyond the limits of the typical mandated school curriculum, we have been challenged to help our children continue their learning, and in so doing, we have also discovered the joys of learning. Like teachers who have found that individualized reading instruction really motivates children to read, we have discovered that allowing our children to learn according to their individual interests motivates learning better than any specialized curriculum. We also found that we don't need years of training to do this work effectively; we simply need to be open to the personal motivations of each of our children.

As I have worked within the schools, I have come to believe that the benefits of homeschooling can be brought to the classrooms of America. Take my sixth graders and their study of Egypt, for example. If teachers were encouraged to go beyond the bounds of such a confined unit of study and instead open it up to the more global idea of studying ancient culture, what then? What if we, as teachers, were free to let that study range over a year, allowing children to study ancient cultures in ways that interested them? Some children might work together to learn about Egypt, while others might study ancient Native American culture, or some particular aspect of another ancient culture. Children who liked math might enjoy exploring the history of mathematics, while children who enjoy sports might like learning about sports activities of the ancients. If education were structured in such a fashion, I believe that more children would enjoy school.

Of course, such a small change in the classroom would mean a dramatic change in the role of teachers. In such classrooms, teachers could not possibly teach everything that individually-paced students want to learn. As a result, teachers would become facilitators of their students' learning experiences, finding mentors within the community to help their students learn. Children would come into contact with adults who could engender a love of learning. In this manner, schooling and homeschooling would become almost indistinguishable from one another — learning environments where the needs of the individual and the pace of learning drive the educational system, and not vice-versa.

These ideas take us far from the story of my work as a teacher and a homeschooling parent. The point is this: by homeschooling our children, our family is considered to be on the fringe of society, yet what we do cannot be overlooked. To help keep individualized, meaningful instruction alive in our schools, I have dedicated myself to working with those students that come my way. Most of the time, I have great difficulty accomplishing my goals; like other teachers, I must help students master the curriculum that is mandated. In a larger context, though, I bring a different vision of education to my work: a vision which questions pre-paced curriculum and the need to standardize everything that children do. Through my work, I can hope that my students will understand that education can be more than worksheets, textbooks and exams. Through my work, I can hope to impart the spirit that education is a cooperative venture, in which students learn from teachers, teachers learn from students, students learn from other students, and teachers learn from one another. I am committed to bringing the ideals and methods of homeschooling into the institution of school. By so doing, I hope to inspire my students to look beyond their classrooms to a future in which they will be in charge of their own learning.

⁓ Chapter 10 ⁓

Learning To Trust In Our Children

Christian and Georgina and I did our morning chores. While we worked, I'd chant my little mantra to myself — "show me the way, show me the way" — and I'd feel confident that, for just that day, just that one day, I'd be able to follow my own advice.

I'LL SAY IT ONCE AGAIN: the most difficult task in our unschooling experience has been learning to trust in our children's natural inclinations to learn. As parents of infants, we were confident that we could provide our children with a safe and loving home. In those early years, we nurtured their sense of curiosity by playing with them and including them in the day-to-day business of family life. In that environment, Christian and Georgina readily learned to walk, talk, and, with our guidance and protection, interact with the larger, unfamiliar world beyond the protective walls of our home.

But, as our children got older and began to demonstrate interest in reading and other subjects taught in school, David and I began to lose confidence that we could provide for their educational needs. However, our commitment to homeschooling forced us to try to better understand why we were feeling less capable as parents when our children reached school age.

I thought of my childhood. My mother had always taken an active part in helping me learn many basic skills, from riding a two-wheel bicycle to deciphering the alphabet. I fondly remembered her encouraging my sister and me to memorize the alphabet; when we did, Mom rewarded us with little wooden zebras, which we proudly displayed on our mantelpiece. She read to us and listened to us read to her. Was my response to Christian's first attempts to read much different? No! Was I much different from my mother or mothers of earlier generations, who helped their children with the rudiments of reading, writing and the like, without worries about doing it right or wrong? I doubted it. Surely I could do as my mother and other mothers had done. What was the worry, then? Where was it coming from?

I thought about the first time I read John Holt's teaching that the ability to learn was something all of us are born possessing. I felt as if I'd discovered a magical truth. I was smitten by the possibility of freeing my children from the regimented structure of a schooled life. As I educated myself about homeschooling, and talked to David about what I was learning, we found ourselves being drawn to Holt's message. His words of solid encouragement and sound reasoning helped us gain self-confidence as learners and parents. His ideas challenged what we'd been taught to believe about how children learn. They challenged us to see our children in a new light — as learners who could be trusted to educate themselves and find their way in this world. Holt's ideas made such good sense to us that we began to seriously commit our family to homeschooling. Why then did our worries resurface when our children came of school age, ready to embark on more traditional learning ventures?

The answer came over the course of our homeschooling experience. It seemed to us that society had changed a great deal since we were children. Unlike our parents, we were under great pressure to see that our children had every possible educational advantage. When David and I were little, it was rare for children to be sent to nursery school, even when, as in David's case, mothers were working. And if children were in nursery school, it was only for a few hours a week, and the emphasis was generally on play rather than "learning." But by the time Christian was born, things had changed radically. "Nursery schools" were out and "preschools" were becoming more common. This was a direct result of more mothers, like myself, entering the work force. More working parents felt pressure to find good preschools for their children, worried that, without preschool experience, children might not do as well in school as expected. Nobody wanted his or her child to be at the dreaded "competitive disadvantage." No wonder David and I had initial feelings of self-doubt: here we were pursuing a "deviant" path! We certainly felt these social pressures to do our best by our children. Wouldn't we "ruin" Christian or Georgina if we should, heaven forbid, teach them "incorrectly?" Just when our "pre-school" children were most actively involved in teaching themselves, society expected us to bundle them up and send them off to school for "proper" instruction.

Over the years of following our own more natural paths of learning, we had ample proof that children are indeed born with a desire to learn. We had come to see that constraints and mandated time-line expectations on traditionally-schooled children often undermined their desire to embrace learning as the adventure it can be. Of course, learning to trust ourselves to live an unschooled life is difficult to do — but ours is a testament to the fact that it can be done.

No curriculum!

For us, letting go of old ideas about teaching, and trusting in our children's sense of direction, was slow and difficult. David and I had both been well-indoctrinated by educational traditions that said children don't know how to learn, aren't interested in learning, and won't learn unless adults take them by the hand and force them to learn. How could we establish curriculum, define subject matter, and select textbooks?

Ultimately, it was Georgina — who continually studied subjects that would not be recognized by the educational establishment — who has done more to help David and me understand the stupidity of trying to box and label learning. As a young girl, Georgina developed a keen interest in animals and swimming. She spent hours each day swimming and doing volunteer swim instruction at the YMCA, and still more hours volunteering at a local pet store. Nothing in our combined educational experience helped us label such activity with recognizable educational terminology. We began to worry: shouldn't Georgina be reading more, or writing science reports, or studying mathematics? Everything David and I had been taught said she should be working at such things, but nothing in her unschooled life presented opportunity for such activities. In fact, mentioning the possibility that she might read or do some math seemed to sour her mood considerably.

These nagging concerns made us wonder whether Georgina's time spent volunteering at the pet store was simply time wasted or time gaining valuable experience. What did she do there? The list was eye-opening. Georgina had been helping price products, cleaning animal cages, arranging sale displays, caring for animals, taking inventory, making independent decisions about what work needed doing when nobody was there, and waiting on customers who wanted animal care products. Georgina told us that when business was slow, she spent time talking with the owners about the joys and woes of running a retail store, keeping customers satisfied, and remaining a profitable endeavor. Although

David and I didn't label Georgina's experience "business education," this was what it was. Georgina was certainly becoming well-versed in the real world of business, and her experiences would enable her to run her own business if she chose to do so in the future.

But what about all the time she spent at the YMCA? What was she doing there to further her learning? She was helping with child care, assisting in the pre-school swim classes, watching the desk when paid staff took short breaks, befriending and helping developmentally-disabled patrons who regularly swam at the Y, participating on the swim team. As we thought about all of these activities, we couldn't think of an educationally-suitable label. Yet there was great value in everything she was doing. She was developing childcare skills, teaching skills, receptionist skills, skills which enabled her to converse with people who are more difficult to understand, and wonderful team spirit. It seemed to us that Georgina was learning skills very useful in the *real* world.

Although the activities of our children, as I have described them throughout this book, indicate that neither child spent hours grappling with traditional curriculum content, each *was* becoming exposed quite naturally to such subjects. The difficulty was ours: we had to learn to look beyond labels to understand this. As we dissected Georgina's and Christian's experiences, we discovered that social studies, math, science, language arts, music, reading, and health could not be separated out as distinct subjects of study in our children's unschooled lives. In fact, what had been misleading us, and caused us to distrust our children's natural inclinations to learn, had been our need to apply subject matter labels to their ever-boundless learning ventures. When we finally understood this, it became much easier for us to let go of our worries and trust that our children would fare well no matter what they chose to do.

No evaluative tools!

David and I also wrestled with how to evaluate our children's progress and achievements in their natural learning process. We couldn't pull out completed workbooks, report cards, test scores, or narrative teacher evaluations to document progress as we had been used to in our own educational upbringings. Instead, we developed our own sort of evaluation process: discussions with one another. When either of us felt uncomfortable with the direction our children were taking, David and I found ourselves in long conversations with one another. These conversations, over time, developed into a natural and almost predictable series of questions about where our children were at the present time in comparison to where they had been a day, a week, a month, six months, or a year ago. Where did they seem to be heading? Were they emotionally stable and happy? And, most importantly, were they interested in learning new and interesting things? As we discussed these concerns, our doubts were put in a more reasonable perspective.

On the simplest level, we often discussed whether or not the children had to "finish" learning projects, especially projects that resembled traditional schoolwork. For example, often one or the other of them would ask us to provide them with books to supplement their work. At this point, I'd give myself a pat on the back and tell myself that this was a true sign that my children were going to learn something of real value. In the back of my mind, I think I wished that my kids would want me to provide more workbooks. Workbooks would make my job of having to provide for their learning needs much simpler!

But this almost never happened. The workbook would be used once or twice, probably for an hour or two on the day that it was new, and maybe in the following week or so. After the newness wore off, Christian or Georgina would put the book aside and change direction. This was my signal to get on my old soapbox and ask them to continue working in the book until it was done. And, like any child, they'd inevitably protest, saying the it was boring, or they didn't need it anymore, or that they didn't want to. With a little more pressure from me they might churn out a page or two more, but that would be the end of it.

At such times, all my lack of faith would surface. I'd begin doubting everything we were doing because my previous ideas about learning said that workbooks had to be finished. As my doubts would get the best of me, I'd turn to David and we'd begin our conversation. What had replaced the workbook activity? Usually, we'd find it had been replaced by something more interesting: reading a different book, skimming through a magazine, building a new Legomobile, collecting leaves, writing an imaginative story, or anything else that would catch their fancy. Whatever the reason, we could usually point to something new on the horizon and understand that leaving the workbook was a healthy choice.

For our children, leaving an activity, even if "unfinished," was always because they had found the energy to take off in yet another direction. In their unschooled lives, notions of "being finished" or "failing" were often irrelevant, unlike us, whose schooled backgrounds had clearly taught us that "not finishing" was often "failing." For years, David and

I had to remind ourselves that learning has no failures, no beginnings and no ends — it simply continues.

No regular lessons!

Georgina's approach to learning to read, as we've seen, was unconventional and yet so intuitively right for her. And one day, it dawned on me that Georgina's reading patterns were similar to mine! I am neither a fast reader nor do I enjoy reading for hours on end. My eyes lose focus and my concentration wanders. David, on the other hand, reads for hours on end, oblivious to the world. And — surprise! — Christian's reading patterns are similar to David's. This realization helped us see that individuals have innately different learning styles and needs.

During our earliest years as parents of unschooled children, David and I spent many an evening discussing whether — and by how much — to allow our children to be in control of the pace of their own learning. We had little idea of what a naturally-paced rhythm of learning was. In our "educated" opinion, the idea that it would take eight years for our daughter to learn to read might be reason to believe that our child was failing. But, in our daughter's mind, learning to read over the course of eight years bore no such meaning. For her, she was simply learning to read. Likewise, when Christian would spend days working on his habitat study and then give it up to spend days immersed in reading a novel, David and I found ourselves at our wit's end. Our educational training told us that Christian should spend some time each day working on his habitat and some time each day reading. But we learned. Georgina's slow and steady pace teaching herself to read kept her so interested in reading that she took her skills beyond anything we could have imagined. And Christian's sporadic studies of his habitat in Owen Park, laced with long intervals of reading, kept him so interested in learning that he later went on to study the nature of streams and fish with unimagined vigor. Had David and I insisted that our children learn according to our preconceived notions of appropriate timelines, they might never have discovered their own capabilities as actor and fly fishing expert.

Show me the way

Often, as David and I get ready for bed, we find ourselves discussing our children's learning.

"David, this morning I was trapped in the same snare. Christian and Georgina were busy playing with Legos, things were going beautifully, and then suddenly there I was, in the center of a mess. I suggested they take the dog for a walk, and then I said, 'When Dickens is walked, Christian, you and I can look over that math you were working on the other day.' Well, you can imagine what happened — melt down! I know we said we weren't going to interfere, but it's been so long since he's done anything."

With such words, we'd find ourselves launched into yet another discussion of how unschooling was supposed to work. Sometimes we felt as though we were going round in circles. We knew we wanted them to learn at their own pace, and yet we'd find ourselves being derailed by the same old worries about curriculum, evaluation and pacing. But no matter what the situation, we always came away from such discussions assured that our children were still learning, despite all our worrying. Trying to keep that simple yet beautiful fact in mind as I drifted off to sleep, I'd repeat, over and over, "show me the way, show me the way" — because I understood so clearly that, indeed, I didn't really yet know where the unschooling path was, how to pick it up, or how to really follow it.

Then come morning, I'd give myself silent reminders to let Christian and Georgina "show me the way." As we all breakfasted together, we'd talk about the day's plans. David might mention that he planned to walk to the yoga center during his lunch hour, or that he might not be home until quite late because of rapidly approaching grant-writing deadlines. Georgina often talked about her friends and which ones she wanted to call. Christian would likely tell us about how he wanted to spend time building his current model or playing with his slingshot. When neither child mentioned reading, writing or math, I'd bite my tongue and remind myself that I wanted them to show me the way. If playing with friends, model building or slingshot practice were what my children desired to do I'd do my best to help them. When breakfast was over and David had departed to catch his bus, Christian and Georgina and I did our morning chores. While we worked, I'd chant my little mantra to myself — "show me the way, show me the way" — and I'd feel confident that, for just that day, just that one day, I'd be able to follow my own advice.

Recognizing the traps

Eventually, David and I did become skilled at recognizing "what went wrong." Almost every time, it was rooted in our compulsion to teach our children those subjects that we'd been taught in school. With great effort, we worked to unleash ourselves from the notion that we had to "teach" our children those things that they naturally showed interest in teaching themselves.

Learning to trust our children's natural instinct to learn began in their preschool years. At that time, we were delighted to witness their language skills develop from babbling, to mimicking sounds, to using pre-language sounds: when Christian stood in front of the refrigerator, pointing and saying, "Ma, ma, ma," we knew he was telling us he was thirsty. Later, when Christian and Georgina were learning skills commonly taught only in school, David and I tried to remind ourselves of that picture of Christian standing in front of the refrigerator, pointing his tiny finger and saying, "Ma, ma, ma." Our belief that Christian would someday be able to ask us for juice or milk helped us trust that Georgina would someday understand and be able to read the letters that spelled "G-e-o-r-g-i-n-a." Over time, and with conscious effort, we came to believe that just as our preschool children had learned to walk and talk, they would learn to read and write. When we worried about whether or not Georgina's pace for learning to read was too slow, we reminded ourselves of her first words and how she'd turned them into complex sentences.

As time went on, David and I came to see that learning really was a natural part of the growth and development of all children. Over time, we learned to put aside our assumptions about how to teach "things taught in school," and began to think in terms of "things that are interesting to learn." As this transformation took place, David and I began to understand how beautifully learning and interest could be integrated. Georgina was learning, quite painlessly, how to alphabetize as she used the card catalogue to find books on apes, orangutans and pigs. We didn't have to create a "lesson" for her to learn this skill, because, just as she needed to communicate with us, she needed to use the card files at the library. Christian was learning similar lessons as he sought to learn all he could about fly fishing and fly-tying. There was no need to create lessons to teach our children things they wanted to master. What we had to learn was how to facilitate our children's learning.

We become learning facilitators

As students who attended school from kindergarten through college, David and I most often were the passive recipients of our teachers' knowledge. Rarely did we take an active role in creating a learning environment that would nourish our own curiosity. But when we became homeschooling parents, we found ourselves thrust into an active learning environment unlike anything we'd ever experienced before.

David and I floundered in this environment for quite some time. There were no titles, school board decisions, or curriculum demands to shield us from giving anything but an honest answer to their questions. To say to them, "We had to do this, so we think it might be good for you to do it too," was just not good enough. Confronted by such truths, we set out to become facilitators, rather than directors, of learning.

Of course, we knew a lot about our community and its resources. Beginning with simple things like a trip to the park or the library, we introduced them to the daily activities of community life. As they got older, they began to develop their own interests in community life. To help them make appropriate connections, we made phone calls, talked with acquaintances, used the yellow pages, talked to reference librarians, or local businessmen. This method of inquiry soon became standard procedure. As they grew older, our children took over the entire process of researching and finding community connections whenever they felt the urge to explore new interests.

New interests often required different sorts of facilitating. Sometimes Christian or Georgina simply needed materials. For example, when Christian was eight, he developed a fascination with dissection. Where could we find things to dissect? I turned to our local librarian. She directed us to some books that she thought might be useful. We leafed through them and sent for various specimen catalogues that I thought might serve Christian's purposes. Once the catalogues arrived, Christian and I sat down and looked over the offerings, decided on a budget, and ordered specimens for dissection that fit within our budget and seemed to meet his needs. Once the specimens arrived, Christian, David, and Georgina began studying the library books describing dissection techniques, and then they moved from reading about dissection to actual dissection.

We also found specialized classes to enrich their blossoming interests; after-school classes, soccer teams, summer enrichment classes, and tutors all became part of our children's larger learning environment. The expenses of this sort of activity were always a concern to us, and in many instances our children were asked to pitch in and help pay the cost of such classes and lessons. In so doing, they learned valuable lessons about choosing wisely and planning their expenses.

Each time our children explored new learning paths, David and I were challenged to let their curiosity be our guide. There were no textbooks to tell us how to do it. Instead, we had to trust our instincts and let our children show us the way. Having lived through it, we can now say that the experiment was a success. We strongly believe that any child can experience similar success if parents and other community members support the child's inquisitiveness and believe in an educational method in which personal discovery serves as the primary vehicle for learning.

⚜ Chapter 11 ⚜

Reflections

The question, "How can you be sure that you know how to teach every-thing a child needs to know?" had become a non-question in our life.

WHEN DAVID AND I DECIDED TO KEEP CHRISTIAN out of kindergar-ten, we hoped that he would not lose his enthusiasm for learning. Chris-tian and Georgina, like all young children, were innately curious about their world, and we wanted to keep that curiosity alive as long as pos-sible. We reasoned that, if we kept them free of institutional constraints about what they must learn, when they must learn it, and how long they must study any particular subject, they would continue to be enthusi-astic about learning. Such a simple idea!

Learning to trust

Today, as we look back on what we set out to do, we can see that we didn't even come close to comprehending the magnitude of it. We didn't understand the implications of such an undertaking, nor were we aware of how deeply we had been affected by the educational practices we had grown up with. Trusting our children to select their own learning paths was not easy — nor has it been fully realized. Today, as in 1983, we worry about how to provide appropriate limits and needed protections, while encouraging them to grow in their understanding of the world.

Even though my work in public schools reminded us how stifling school bells, school curriculum, and 8:00 to 3:00 school days could be, freeing ourselves from the grip of those "standard" educational practices was more difficult than either of us ever imagined. We were fortunate that in moments of crisis, we could turn to our resources: our children, our readings *(Growing Without Schooling, Home Education Magazine,* John Holt's, Nancy Wallace's, and David and Micki Colfax's books, among others), and our support group network. Over the years, we came to know that our children's desires to learn were far greater than our ability to label them and confine them to traditional categories of learning. As we came to understand this truth, we learned to trust in our children and follow their lead. In the end, *they* became the ones who taught us about the simple beauty of living and learning.

Talking about homeschooling

In talking to people about the homeschooled life, we have encountered both outright attack and heartfelt praise for our efforts. Each situation provided us with new windows of understanding through which to view our own circumstances. No longer are we cautious about explaining to people how our children follow a curriculum based upon their individual lives and not a curriculum mandated by the public school system. We tell the curious that our children, and many others like them, have become socialized — in the midst of dirty dishes, sibling squabbles, family vacations, and late night discussions — and have found ways to master knowledge important to their unique interests. Although we understand why people worry about textbooks, curriculum guidelines, diplomas, and the like, we hope that learning about our family's homeschooled life will help others realize that they, too, are capable of living and learning alongside their children.

Educating education students about homeschooling

For the past ten years, our family has been asked to present our experiences as a homeschooling family to students in a class entitled "School and Society," taught by Professor of Education Vern Haubrich, at the University of Wisconsin, Madison. Recently, as I prepared for another presentation to this class, I was struck by how far we had come since I first visited that classroom.

In 1985, when Christian was seven and Georgina three, I made my first presentation in Vern's class. I went alone, and I was quite nervous and didn't know what to expect. David and I talked about the possibility that I might face hostility from both the students and the professor. As I walked into the classroom that morning, I wondered if I was entering the enemy's camp. Could I do justice to myself and other homeschoolers? Could I speak up without becoming defensive? Would I feel comfortable enough to talk about what our children were *really* doing — that they were learning *without* using curriculum and textbooks that these students were being trained to think were necessities for proper education?

I had come prepared to answer questions about our motivation to homeschool, about our "curriculum" and about "socialization." The students did ask these questions and I offered answers that I thought were responsive. I talked about what I saw as the pitfalls of institutionalized education: problems that arise when children are segregated by age, the negative impact of an educational system based on a formula where teachers ask the questions and students answer, the outcome that most children learn that asking questions, rather than being a mark of intelligence, is a mark of stupidity, and so forth. I was taken aback, though, by one question at the end of the hour: "How can you and David be sure that you know how to teach everything that a child needs to know?"

I'd heard that question from parents many times before, but here I was, in the midst of a classroom full of students who appeared to have no real understanding of what I had just spent forty-five minutes talking about! They seemed unable to grasp that there is no possible way that David or I, or any teacher or textbook, could know (much less teach) all that our children need to know. These students, soon to be teachers, were trapped in the belief that all there is to learn can be put in lesson plans, labeled and doled out at appropriate times. Unable to think that learning could occur outside the scope of curriculum, these students seemed wedded to a belief that without a complete set of particular pieces of information imparted by teachers, children may never succeed in this world.

I had naively assumed that by briefly describing our homeschooling experiences to these future educators, they would readily understand a truth that had taken us years to absorb: that learning is an undefinable and limitless adventure. These students still believed that organized education — with its textbooks and curriculum — contained the holy truth, and that with these tools teachers could teach all that students need to know. In the moment that it took me to realize this, I finally understood how far out on a limb we had gone. Our family was living educational reforms that others, like these students, had not even been able to envision. The question, "How can you be sure that you know how to teach everything a child needs to know?" had become a non-question in our life. Slowly, without our realizing it, we had discovered a profound truth about education: we didn't need to know everything, we simply had to have a desire to help one another learn together.

At this first meeting with the students in Vern's class, I tried to turn the question back to the class: "How can you be sure that you know the sum total of what it is my children need to know?" A room full of blank faces stared at me; a few of the more vocal students attempted to warn me that we could be damaging our children by not teaching them "everything" that schools taught. As the class was ending, I asked them if they remembered the sum total of what they had learned in first, sixth, or tenth grade. Some belated nods of understanding suggested that maybe a few of the prospective teachers in the class might have begun to get the message of my homeschooling story.

Over the years I returned to Vern's class many times, and each presentation reflected our current homeschooling experiences. Sometimes I went alone and at other times some or all of our family accompanied me. We became very comfortable presenting our story and generally felt welcome. My first presentation was at a time when David and I were still struggling with our own doubts about the unschooling process. Then, our experience with unschooling was so limited I couldn't be sure of anything. Our children were simply too young to be the "proof of the pudding" yet. But as the years passed, and we experienced success with unschooling, our presentations became easier to give. Each time we went, we simply told about our current experiences. One year I'd speak about letting Georgina learn to read at her own pace, and how allowing her to do so maintained her enthusiasm for learning despite being unable to read as well as most eight-year-olds. The next year we might talk about Christian's lack of interest in anything traditionally academic. This topic brought up questions about learning traditional subject matter and gave us the opportunity to show how Christian's everyday life included science, math, reading and history.

A parting lesson

Professor Haubrich was retiring. On the day of our last meeting with his students, Georgina, Christian and I walked into a very full classroom. I was gratified to know that the concept of homeschooling was no longer considered to be on the lunatic fringe; this was confirmed when the two young women who presented us to the class began by summarizing the history of homeschooling law, the Wisconsin homeschooling law, and the writings of John Holt.

Then, after they introduced us, I gave the class a synopsis of our homeschooling history. I began by telling the students that what I had come to say would probably be difficult to comprehend. "When we set out to homeschool, we did so because we wanted our children to be the guides of their own learning. We wanted them to be free to learn about whatever it was that interested and intrigued them." In the next forty minutes, I told them the basic story of this book, hoping to convey the complexity of attempting to live a life free of preconceived notions of learning.

The students had many questions, such as, "Tell us about your typical day, when do the kids study?" My answer was that today was a "typical day": we were doing what the day demanded. We woke up, had breakfast, got ready to come to this class, and from here would be going for hair cuts, lunch and then home where Christian would tie flies or read until it was time to deliver the newspapers on his route, and Georgina would probably meet her friend at the pool and swim for the afternoon.

One of the questions was the standard one, "What about socialization?" When we had entered the classroom that spring morning, I had noticed that one of the students was one of Georgina's YMCA camp counselors from the previous summer. Nodding to the familiar young man sitting across the room, whose name I did not know, I said, "I would like to turn this question over to you because you know my daughter from Y camp." Although I had told the class that "socialization" was really not an issue, here was a ready-made opportunity for corroboration. He said, "Georgina was at Y camp for two weeks. Everyone seemed to like her and she got along with kids of all ages. She didn't stand out as being any different from any other camper." I couldn't have asked for a better testimonial.

As the class concluded, I felt a little sad knowing that we wouldn't be coming back to talk to future classes, but the sadness I felt made me realize that I'd grown. I no longer worried about coming to the "enemy camp" to talk about homeschooling and, in fact, I enjoyed being a part of these classes. While the students packed their bags and went on their way, a few students remained to ask a final question or two.

One woman asked me, "How old is your son?"

"Fifteen," I answered.

"That's amazing. He's never gone to school and yet he spoke with such ease in our class. I'm just beginning to feel confident enough to speak in my seminars — and I know everyone. He didn't know anyone here, and yet he jumped in whenever he had something to say."

I was caught off guard to hear words of praise for such ordinary behavior, so it took me a second or two before I could say, "Well, you see, Christian and Georgina's lives are spent learning things from many others, not from a single teacher. That's why they have no hesitation about speaking up when they come here to talk. They are simply doing what they have done all their lives: participating in learning."

At this moment, a man who was standing in the group said, "That's why Christian could become a radio engineer at thirteen. No one ever told him he was too young to consider doing the work. He's grown up doing things when he felt ready to do them. He's not waiting for someone to tell him he is old enough or knows enough to do particular tasks. This means that he is *really* living in our community."

This statement took my breath away. Here, in a nutshell, was an expression of what David and I had so often been unable to see right before our eyes: unschooling does work in simple yet beautiful ways. What this man had said revealed to me that, indeed, our children had already made a very natural and easy transition into living "in the real world" on their own terms. Although we thought of Christian and Georgina as being a part of "the real world," what we had failed to appreciate was that they were now a part of that world quite independent of us.

The imaginary threshold

Once again our traditional educational backgrounds had persuaded us to think that our children would *become* productive community members only when they "grew up," and we had been waiting for that time to arrive before allowing ourselves to declare our unschooling a success. But this comment, coming at the end of our final classroom visit, made us see that our children *are* productive community members *now*. I realized that because our society keeps children in school until they "graduate" at age eighteen, I still had the belief that at eighteen something magical would happen and a transition into community life would begin. Here I was, fully committed to homeschooling, and yet I had been waiting for our children to cross that invisible threshold and enter into the "real world" of adults. What I had missed was that no such threshold existed for Christian or Georgina or other unschooled children. I had failed to see that, as we unschooled our children, we had been integrating them into the life of our community. Our children were certainly not waiting to become involved in community life — they were already in it! It took this stranger's comment about Christian, "that he is *really* living in our community," to make me fully see the genuine beauty of unschooling: that it is the most natural and failsafe way to educate children whose learning begins the day they are born and knows no limits.

Christian and Georgina had completed many of the most natural of life transitions without our being aware of them. Small first steps like trips to the library, or working alongside Mom at the co-op enabled both children to safely explore the larger world beyond the bounds of home. As their comfort with people of all ages grew, they made their own inroads into community life through volunteer work. Both children made their own friends and acquaintances. As their interests grew beyond what David or I could help them with, they turned to tutors and mentors for support. Working alongside people from all walks of life, they learned what they needed. For them, no diploma could mark the beginnings of a meaningful life, for both children had lived meaningful lives from the outset.

Unlike their parents, Christian and Georgina didn't grow up expecting a high school diploma to usher them into the adult world. Rather, their lives have been an ongoing process of self-evaluation and gradual initiation into the adult world. With no artificial limits to their participation, they have already found their places in our community as capable young people, and have already made real contributions to it. They need no diploma to mark their entry into the adult world because, in fact, they have never been separated from it.

⸙ Chapter 12 ⸙

Epilog

"Do I regret not having gone to a regular school? No. Many schooled kids haven't ever learned things that interest them. I've been lucky that way. My life has been great — I wouldn't want to change it."

— Christian McKee

IN LESS THAN THREE DAYS, Christian will be leaving home for the summer. Because of his fly-tying skills, he's been invited to work for six weeks for a fly-fishing business near Yellowstone National Park in Montana. Although he's been away for short periods before, this will be the first time he will be living independently, supporting himself through a skill he taught himself. And after his stint in Montana, he'll spend another six weeks as a counselor teaching German at Concordia Language Villages in Bemidji, Minnesota. In the fall, he'll be heading off to Kalamazoo College (a small liberal arts college in Michigan), thanks to his interesting application for admission, solid test scores, generous scholarships, financial aid, and, of course, a bit of our savings.

Today we're sitting in his bedroom, helping him pack. We're sad to see him go, but we're proud of all he's accomplished. We talk of this and that, but underneath we're very aware that he's moving on, out of childhood. Like all parents at moments like this, we wonder: Did we do everything we could have done for him? Did we do the right thing to homeschool him? Will he be well-prepared for the future? After a while, David asks him if he ever regrets not having gone to a regular school.

"No. Many schooled kids haven't ever learned things that interest them. I've been lucky that way. My life has been great — I wouldn't want to change it."

What more could we ask?

A walk and a talk in the park

While Christian continues his packing, David and I go for a walk in a nearby park and find ourselves talking about our feelings about Christian's imminent departure. Soon our conversation becomes yet another discussion about our homeschooling experience.

"You know, Alison," David says, "the breadth and depth of Christian's and Georgina's achievements are quite amazing. They've mastered reading, writing, and math, of course, but that's not all. It's what they've accomplished beyond the scope of a traditional education that's so amazing to me — they've both taken their learning far beyond the limits of what we expected, given our own traditional education. What I mean is, they've naturally learned how to communicate effectively, and how to take on and finish tasks. Most importantly, they've learned how to find joy in learning."

"Yes," I told him, "I'm so happy they've both done so well — but we can't forget that there have been costs, too. Financially, we've sacrificed the benefits of a dual income to be with them. In the early years, we relied on the WIC supplemental food program — we weren't too proud to accept free surplus food then, either. Homeschooling has meant shopping at garage sales and Goodwill when our income was low, going without family vacations, and having to give up a lot of things that other families seem to have."

"That's true. And don't forget we've never had any 'time off' either, like a lot of parents whose children are in school during the day. Being full-time parents has been more than either of us expected. We've had to be careful all the time, always balancing our own relationship with the needs of the kids."

"Do you think Christian really understands why we did all this, David? Although he says he wouldn't trade his life for a schooled life, he's had his share of complaints along the way. When we were helping him write his 'prose transcript' for college admission, remember how he wished he could simply ask a school counselor for a transcript?"

"Yes, but remember how he felt at the end of the week? He said, 'Wow, I've really done a lot these past five years, haven't I?' No doubt it's been hard for him at times always to have to chart his own way, but look what he's gained. Look at who he is, at how confident he is, especially around adults. None of that would have been possible without the tremendous variety of experiences he's had."

"David, I know Georgina seems to know instinctively that this is the best route for her, too. But she's so social. We often wonder whether having access to more friends in a regular school setting wouldn't be better for her."

"But, Alison, every time she really thinks about it, she decides that she doesn't want to be in school, especially when she hears her friends complain about classes they don't like, homework they don't want to do, and teachers they don't like. She always claims that being with people of all ages is much more interesting than being cooped up with her same-age friends all day! How many times have we heard her say, 'School would be a waste of my time!'"

We walked on in silence. Then David asked me, "Alison, when you think about our homeschooling experience, what comes to mind? What's it all been about?"

"Well, you know, for me, it's been a spiritual journey, too. Through this experiment, we've discovered the real meaning of trust. For me, homeschooling has become a way of making the world a safe and accessible place for our children to live and learn. They grew and matured inside the cocoon we made for them, and now our firstborn is about to break out of the cocoon and fly away."

"Well, I have to agree with you. I mean, here he is, off to Montana for a summer of fly fishing and fly-tying. Who would have imagined that, on the day he came out of his room to tell us he wanted to learn about ice-fishing, it would lead to all this?"

By this time, we have reached the end of the trail and we head slowly down the hill. As we enter the greenway behind our home, we see Christian and Georgina playing a game of Frisbee together. I'm immediately struck by the thought (as any mother would be at a time like this) that our two children will not have many more times like this together. Although I have tears in my eyes, I am also deeply grateful for having been able to share so much of their lives.

In silence, David and I watch Christian and Georgina for a time, and then go into the house together.

ᵈᵉ Appendix 1 ᵉᵈ

Books About Children & Learning

OVER THE YEARS OUR FAMILY HAS READ QUITE A LOT about alternatives in education. Listed below are some of our favorites; this should give you a good starting point. Many of the titles listed are available from *Growing Without Schooling*. You can also consult your library for more titles.

A word of advice

Whenever you encounter reference to specific legal aspects of homeschooling, remember that each state has different laws governing homeschooling. Many sources purport to outline the legal requirements for homeschooling state-by-state, but I have often found misleading information regarding homeschooling laws. Before making any decisions about homeschooling, consult the statutes regulating homeschooling, grass roots organizations involved with homeschooling issues in your area and state, and support groups and experienced homeschoolers.

Books

Colfax, David and Micki. *Hard Times in Paradise.*
This is the story of how the Colfax family was driven from their home and community because of their political views and how they came to live in a remote northern California community where schools were too far away for their children to attend. Included is the story of how the first three of their four sons got into Harvard — and much, much more.

Colfax, David and Micki. *Homeschooling for Excellence.*
The story of the Colfax family and their homeschooling experiences. Resources that they found useful are listed.

Gatto, John Taylor. *Dumbing Us Down.*
A compilation of essays based on speeches by educator John Taylor Gatto, including his discussion of the lessons schools teach our children. He makes a strong argument for less, rather than more, schooling.

Guterson, David. *Family Matters: Why Homeschooling Makes Sense.*
In this book, Guterson, then a high school English teacher and now a noted novelist, discusses the reasons he and his wife chose to homeschool their children, the pros and cons of homeschooling, and many other issues of the homeschooling movement, such as its history, homeschooling laws, homeschoolers' financial concerns, socialization, the parent/teacher role, and much more. It is an in-depth and clearly written study that presents the pros and cons of school and home-school from the point of view of a person who lives in both worlds.

Hegener, Mark and Helen (eds.). *Alternatives In Education.*
A compilation of articles dealing with alternatives in education, the politics of education, homeschooling, alternative schools, Waldorf and Montessori schools, and biographies of many famous alternative educators.

Holt, John. *How Children Fail.*
A thorough discussion of why children fail in school and a plea to educators and other adults to examine their roles in such failures.

Holt, John. *How Children Learn.*
A book devoted to showing parents and educators how children approach learning as a natural process.

Holt, John. *Teach Your Own.*
A discussion of homeschooling, court rulings, and other matters. Answers the most commonly voiced objections to homeschooling. Includes legal advice.

Holt, John. *What Do I Do On Monday?*
A practical discussion of how homeschooling might work in any family.

Kaseman, Susan and Larry. *Taking Charge Through Home Schooling: Personal and Political Empowerment.*
This book provides an analysis of current educational trends and practical advice on how to take charge of the educational needs of your children.

Leistico, Agnes. *I Learn Better By Teaching Myself.*
The story of the Leistico family and how they used a student-directed approach to learning. (When Georgina was nine, I read this book to her and she loved it.)

Leistico, Agnes. *Still Teaching Ourselves.*

This book begins where *I Learn Better By Teaching Myself* left off and follows the Leistico family through high school, college and into the work place.

Neill, A.S. *Summerhill.*

This is the book A.S. Neill wrote about his famous school in England. An excellent beginning point for those interested in exploring alternatives in education.

Pedersen, Anne and Peggy O'Mara (eds.). *Schooling At Home: Parents, Kids and Learning.*

A thorough discussion of homeschooling, including legal issues, methods of teaching, and many personal accounts of homeschooling.

Snitzer, Herb. *Living At Summerhill.*

A photographer's view of Summerhill and the children who were in attendance during A.S. Neill's lifetime.

Wallace, Nancy. *Better Than School.*

My favorite book when we first started homeschooling. This is the story of Nancy's struggle to free their son from a stifling schooling experience and how she and her husband taught both of their children at home.

Wallace, Nancy. *Child's Work: Taking Children's Choices Seriously.*

Nancy's story of learning how to take her young children's interests and choices seriously, continuing (somewhat) where *Better Than School* left off.

·⁓ Appendix 2 ⁓·

Websites, Newsletters, Magazines & Catalogues

THE ITEMS LISTED HERE ARE JUST A SAMPLING of what our family has felt to be most useful; there are many more resources available. Curriculum supplies abound, but since our family has not used much in the way of traditional curriculum, I have refrained from listing materials we have not had personal experience with.

Homeschooling resources

The Drinking Gourd
> P.O. Box 2557, Redmond WA 98073
> www.accesseric.org/resources/parent/homesch2.html
> A multi-cultural magazine that explores homeschooling from different cultural perspectives.

Family Unschoolers Network (F.U.N.)
> 1688 Belhaven Woods Court, Pasadena MD 21122-3727
> www.unschooling.org

The Forum, **National Homeschool Association**
> P.O. Box 157290, Cincinnati OH 45215-7290

Growing Without Schooling
> 2380 Massachusetts Ave., Suite 104, Cambridge MA 02140
> (617) 864-3100
> www.holtgws.com

Home Education Magazine
> P.O. Box 1083, Tonasket WA 98855
> www.home-ed-magazine.com

For a listing of magazines for more specific interests (e.g., a particular religious affiliation, geographic setting, family situation, or educational need), contact Growing Without Schooling.

Miscellaneous web sites

Education World
www.education-world.com/parents/homeschool/index.html

Encyclopedia Britannica
www.britannica.com

Education Hotline
www.gohotline.com/education

Homeschool.com
www.homeschool.com

John's Homeschool Resource Page
www.midnightbeach.com/hs/hem.htm

Lightspan Study Web
www.studyweb.com

State and National Homeschool Groups
www.mhla.org/stateandnational.htm

WebCT — A Learning Hub
www.webct.com

Math and science resources

Cuisenaire Company of America
P.O. Box 5026, White Plains NY 10602-5026
(800) 237-3142
www.cuisenaire.com

Hands-on math materials for all ages

Edmund Scientific Co.
101 East Gloucester Pike, Barrington NJ 08007-1380
www.edsci.com

Key Curriculum Press
P.O. Box 2304, Berkeley CA 94702
(800) 338-7638
www.keypress.com
Clearly written, step-by-step, non-intimidating math workbooks and
books to use with Cuisenaire rods. Appropriate for all ages.

Nasco

901 Janesville Ave., P.O. Box 901, Fort Atkinson WI 53538

www.mascofa.com/prod/HOME

Has a science catalog and a dissection equipment & specimens catalog (plus much more).

National Geographic Society

Washington DC 20036

(800) 447-0647

www.nationalgeographic.com

Has many games and books; ask for any catalogs that may be of interest.

Ranger Rick Magazine

National Wildlife Federation

8925 Leesburg Pike, Vienna VA 22184-0001.

www.nwf.org/rrick

Also: *Your Big Back Yard*, an excellent magazine for very young readers.

Sunburst

101 Castleton St., P.O. Box 100, Pleasantville NY 10570

(800) 321-7511

www.sunburst.com

Complete catalog of computer software that is commonly used in schools. Covers math, science, and language arts. (Software for all computers.) CD-ROM titles also available.

3-2-1 Contact

E=MC Square, P.O. Box 51177, Boulder CO 80321-1177

Zephyr Press

P.O. Box 13448, Tucson AZ 85732-3448

www.zephyrpress.com

Catalog of many books dedicated to developing the multiple intelligences of children. One of our favorites was *A Mathematical Mystery Tour: Higher-Thinking Math Tasks* — and the newspaper that came with it.

Zoobooks

Wildlife Education, Ltd., 3590 Kettner Blvd., San Diego, CA 92101

www.zoobooks.com

Literature resources

Avon Books

1350 Avenue of the Americas, New York NY 10019

Chinaberry Book Service
2780 Via Orange Way, Suite B, Spring Valley CA 91978
(800) 776-2242
www.chinaberry.com
This is our favorite book catalog. It offers book reviews for each title; books are arranged by interest and age level.

Dover Publications (Children's Catalog)
31 East 2nd Street, Mineola NY 11501
www.doverpublications.com
Hundreds of unusual and hard-to-find book titles. Prices as low as $1.00.

Listening Library, Inc.
One Park Avenue, Old Greenwich CT 06870-1727
www.listeninglib.com
Books on tape.

Mind's Eye
Box 1060, Petaluma CA 94953
(800) 227-2020
www.mindseye.vstorestuff.com
Books on tape.

Recorded Books Inc.
270 Skipjack Rd., Prince Frederick MD 20678
(800) 638-1304
www.recordedbooks.com

Scholastic Books
P.O. Box 7502, Jefferson City MO 65102
(800) 325-6149
www.scholastic.com
Scholastic Books has many offerings. Our children participated in their children's book clubs for years and also enjoyed their geography workbooks, newspapers (*Scholastic News*), and magazines.

Miscellaneous catalog resources

Aristoplay
P.O. Box 7529, Ann Arbor MI 48107
(800) 634-7738
www.aristoplay.com
A wonderful assortment of unusual games, ranging from science and history to literature and music. Our children especially enjoyed *Made for Trade: A Game of Early American Life; Music Maestro* (an introduction to music appreciation); *By Jove* (based on Greek Mythology); *The Play's the Thing* (an introduction to Shakespeare); and *True Science.*

Bellerophon Books
36 Anacapa St., Santa Barbara CA 93101
(800) 253-9943
www.bellerphonbooks.com
Coloring books and activity books with historical themes.

Hearthsong
156 N. Main St., Sebastopol CA 95472
(800) 325-2502
www.hearthsong.com
A wonderful assortment of books, toys, arts and crafts equipment, and more. They offer high quality products, which are unique and appropriate for many ages, even teens.

Kids' History Company
P.O. Box 1521, Sonoma CA 95476
A catalog of many difficult-to-find history books. Sound dull? The books are carefully selected with children in mind and the selection is excellent.

Lego, Shop-At-Home Service
555 Taylor Rd., P.O. Box 1310, Enfield CT 06083-1310
(800) 453-4652
www.lego.com
A complete assortment of Lego building sets, many of which are not available in stores.

T.C. Toy
P.O. Box 749, Skaneateles NY 13152
(800) 359-1233
A wonderful assortment of wooden building sets, toys, games and trains for young children.

The Whole Work Catalog
New Careers Center, Inc., 1515 23rd St., P.O. Box 339-CT Boulder CO 80306
A catalog chock-full of books dealing with creative options for alternative careers, self-employment, and home business opportunities.

⚜ Appendix 3 ⚜

Special Interest Resources For Teens

TODAY'S TEENAGERS ARE UNDER SIGNIFICANT SOCIAL PRESSURE not only to get high school diplomas, but also to continue their education in college and to become economically productive citizens. I am including this special appendix for teenagers who may be looking for different paths through life.

Baker, Britt. *Letters Home.*
> A compilation of letters teenager Britt Baker wrote home to her local newspaper as she traveled across the U.S., Canada and Italy doing apprenticeships in various fields of science.

Bear, John. *College Degrees by Mail.*
> Information about colleges that offer degrees through home study; alternative ways to earn college credits; and other useful information a college applicant might want.

Careers and Colleges, **Home Education Press.**
> A compilation of ten articles from *Home Education Magazine* offering advice about college and career choices. Resources are listed.

Gelner, Judy. *College Admissions: A Guide for Homeschoolers.*
> Details of how one homeschooling family got their child into college. Many helpful suggestions regarding how to explain an unschooled child's life to college admission staff.

Graham, Robin Lee. *Dove.*
> The remarkable story of how Robin Graham, at the age of sixteen, set out to sail solo around the world. His journey lasted five years!

Kohl, Herbert. *The Question Is College: Guiding Your Child to the Right Choices After High School.*
> A book that takes a second look at the non-college options for any teenager. Although the author addresses a typically schooled population, his advice is useful to any parent and teen looking at employment options. Highly recommended.

Leistico, Agnes. *I Learn Better By Teaching Myself*

Leistico, Agnes. *Still Teaching Ourselves.*
> A family's experience learning at home using child-directed learning.

Llewellyn, Grace. *Real Lives: Eleven Teenagers Who Don't Go To School.*
> The unique stories of eleven different teenagers who do not go to school. Some never went to school and others left school for various reasons. The stories are quite remarkable. For teens who are just "rising out" (as opposed to dropping out) of school this book and Grace's other book are *musts* to read.

Llewellyn, Grace. *The Teenage Liberation Handbook: How To Quit School And Get A Real Life And Education.*
> As a former educator, Grace tells the story of her personal experience of school and then offers hundreds of examples of how teens can take responsibility for their own learning outside the confines of a school. An empowering book for any teen. (For teens who have just left school, this is *must* reading.)

McKee, Alison. *From Homeschool To College And Work: Turning Your Homeschool Experiences Into College And Job Portfolios.*
> My book details how we wrote a college transcript for our son, based on his non-traditional educational experiences. The prose transcript we created got Christian admitted to Hamline University, Grinnell College, Kalamazoo College, University of Minnesota-Minneapolis, University of Wisconsin-Eau Claire and the University of Wisconsin-Madison. Available from the author.

·≋ Appendix 4 ≋·

Resources Within Your Own Community

Support groups

ONE OF THE MOST IMPORTANT homeschooling resources is a network of people with similar interests. When we first started homeschooling, David and I needed the support of families who were also attempting to unschool their children. Our children would benefit from being with children who were having similar homeschooling experiences. To create a support network, we turned to *Growing Without Schooling* and *Network News*, and began calling people in our area who were listed in their directories. After making a few phone calls, we organized our first support group meeting. Although our first meetings were very informal, within a short time the group began to develop a structure that suited its needs.

If you live in a community with a support group that you feel comfortable in, join it. If, on the other hand, the support group doesn't meet your need — or there isn't a support group — you will greatly benefit by creating your own support network. Here are a few ideas for starting a homeschooling support group:

• Check the *Growing Without Schooling* directory and contact a few different families who live near you.

• Invite a few of those families to your home for a potluck supper.

• Invite some friends to discuss alternatives in education and mention that you are thinking of homeschooling. See where the discussion might lead.

• Place a (free) public service advertisement in a local paper or advertising circular asking people who are interested in discussing educational alternatives and homeschooling to come to a "get acquainted" meeting.

- Contact a state-wide grassroots homeschooling organization and ask them for names and numbers of people in your area who might be interested in forming a support network.
- Read the "pen-pal" columns in *Growing Without Schooling* and *Home Education Magazine* and form a pen-pal support network for parents of children who are pen-pals.
- Correspond with parents who write letters to *Growing Without Schooling* or *Home Education Magazine*.
- Check in on the Internet for homeschooling information and support groups. *Home Education Magazine* has a homeschooling "chatroom" open to all homeschooling families.
- Start a book group that focuses on reading about alternatives in education.
- Check with a local chapter of La Leche League and see if any of the parents in that organization are interested in discussing homeschooling issues.

Finding volunteer opportunities for children

Finding successful volunteer experiences for children can be difficult. Children are rarely expected to take work seriously, and therefore many adults are reluctant to accept anyone younger than sixteen as a volunteer. However, there are a few very simple rules-of-thumb you might follow to help find appropriate volunteer opportunities for your child.
- Don't force your child to do volunteer work.
- Set an example for your child by doing volunteer work yourself (meal programs are a good place to start). Have your child come and work alongside you at your volunteer site.
- Keep your ear attuned to your child's unique interests. These interests will be the key to finding successful volunteer opportunities.
- Don't assume that finding volunteer work is impossible. With enough footwork and exploration, the right volunteer opportunity will come along.
- If your child seems to have no interest in volunteer work and you would like to spark that interest, remember to set an example by becoming a volunteer. Have a discussion with your child about the joys and benefits of volunteer work.
- Help your child understand that his or her unique interests may be served by finding a volunteer opportunity that is aligned with those interests.

- Thoroughly explore the volunteer options in your community. Look for service organizations, small businesses, museums, meal programs, private and public sector work sites, community centers, political campaign headquarters, even a neighbor, to provide opportunities for volunteering. Perfectly-matched volunteer opportunities are rare. It's up to you to find the situation that best fits your child's needs.

- When you locate potential volunteer opportunities, visit work sites and unobtrusively observe the working conditions and the people who work there. This will help you determine whether or not this is a volunteer opportunity you and your child will feel comfortable with.

- After selecting a potential volunteer site, be prepared to convince those in charge of the benefits of having a child do volunteer work. Become your child's advocate and prepare yourself to discuss your child's abilities and interests with adults who may work with your child.

- Talk with your child about what to say when asking to volunteer. Role-play the situation beforehand. Adults will be much more willing to offer your child a volunteer opportunity if your child can speak comfortably and knowledgeably at the "interview."

- Once your child has landed the volunteer work, keep an eye on the situation. Remember that not all adults are familiar with the capabilities of young workers. Remind your child of this. If your child feels that his or her skills are not being adequately utilized, encourage him or her to ask permission to do more challenging jobs. (At the outset, our Georgina had to ask the pet store owners if she could help clean cages and stock shelves. In time, her supervisors simply asked her if she would like to do this or that job. If she felt able, she did it or asked to be taught how to do it.)

- When you talk to your child's potential supervisors, be aware that they may be reluctant to ask your child to work. Be sure to give permission for this and suggest ways in which they might utilize your child's skills. Again, not all adults understand the abilities of children.

- If the volunteer situation does not work out, consider looking elsewhere for similar work. (Christian's first volunteer opportunity at a public radio station failed to be what he wanted it to be. After spending considerable time talking to him and his supervisor, we realized that this particular situation was simply not working. But David checked into another public radio station, and Christian has been volunteering there for five years!) So, don't be afraid to look for other opportunities if your first choice proves incompatible.

• Become knowledgeable about the child-labor laws in your state. All states have restrictions on the minimum age for children to work, and on the number of hours children are permitted to work. Volunteer work (for no pay) may or may not be subject to such restrictions. Many employers, especially small businesses, may not think about this issue when considering giving volunteer opportunities to your child, but you should be aware of it so you can judge if the hours and working conditions are appropriate. (This information is easily obtained from your local library or state representative's office or city hall — and finding out about it could be an interesting research project for your child!)

Appendix 5

Automobile Insurance & College Admissions

Automobile insurance

STUDENTS WHO ATTEND TRADITIONAL SCHOOLS can qualify for discounts on their automobile insurance if they achieve a good grade point average. Each insurance company has different standards for what that GPA should be. In order to qualify, a report card needs to be submitted to the insurance company indicating grades for the current semester and an overall GPA. If you believe your son or daughter would qualify, you can prepare a report card indicating grades and GPA.

When Christian reached driving age, we asked our insurance agent how Christian might qualify. When we mentioned that he was home-schooled, the immediate response was that we'd have to submit test scores or a report card. Of course, we didn't have "official" test scores but since we were legally educating Christian at home, we could issue Christian a report card. This was the only time we ever used grades or class labels. The grades were simply a reflection of how we felt Christian was doing with each project. We considered what Christian was doing and created the following "report card":

<u>BITTERSWEET ACADEMY</u>
Final Grade Report June 1994
Christian Charles McKee

(The notes following each grade were not on the report card. They are added here so that you can see what we were thinking about as we created the document.)

Small Business Methods . . . . **B**
(Christian was running his own fly-tying business at the time)

French 4 . . . . **A**
(Christian was studying with a tutor who felt he would be earning an A if he was in traditional school)

German 6 . . . . **A—**
(This was the grade Christian was earning in a course at the University)

English Literature and Composition . . . . **A**
(Christian was reading lots of literature at the time and working on his writing skills)

Journalism/Mass Communication . . . . **A**
(Christian was volunteering as a radio engineer two nights a week)

Physical Education . . . . **B**
(Christian was delivering two daily papers at the time)

Stream Ecology . . . . **A**
(Christian was spending considerable time fishing at various streams and making note of the health of each stream)

GPA: 3.75 (on a 4.0 scale)

This report card, printed on our home printer on standard paper, met the required needs of our insurance company and qualified Christian for a "good student" discount. (Of course, we would have never applied for such a discount had we had any concerns that Christian wouldn't be a safe driver or that in fact he wasn't a "good student.") This report card truly reflected how we felt Christian was doing.

College admissions

It is a common misconception that homeschoolers will not be able to get into college. A quick perusal of *Growing Without Schooling* and other national magazines and newspapers should assure you that this is not the case. In the past ten or fifteen years, homeschooled children have been getting into colleges across the country quite regularly, many of them Ivy League schools. If and when your young adult declares an interest in attending college, be prepared to team up with him or her to successfully work through the admissions process together.

From the beginning, you must understand that your child's home-schooled background will be both an asset and a liability in the application process. The positive aspect of being homeschooled is that your student will attract the attention of almost all college admissions officers who are always on the lookout for students with interesting and unusual backgrounds. The liability of a homeschooled student's application is that you will have to convince admissions personnel that the applicant can handle college-level work.

How to make a convincing case? First and foremost are the ACT (American College Testing Program) and SAT (Scholastic Aptitude Test) tests. Most colleges and universities require these achievement and aptitude tests. To send for test packets, write to ACT Registration, P.O. Box 414, Iowa City IA 52243-0414; and College Board SAT Program, Princeton NJ 08541. You may also get applications for these tests from local public and private high schools. Getting these common entrance exams out of the way will be the easiest part of the application process.

A few words of advice about taking the SAT and ACT tests

• First, encourage your son or daughter to study well for these tests (the *Princeton Study Guide Books*, available from local book stores, are best for this).

• Discourage taking the tests more than once or twice. In the first place, the tests can be costly to take; but more importantly, it is highly unlikely that test scores will significantly improve from test to test. (I've also been told that admissions officers recognize "test score shopping" and consider this in a negative light when reviewing an applicant's file.)

• "Subject area tests" should also be taken only once. If multiple "subject area tests" are required, plan to take each test on a separate date. This will alleviate stress and allow time to prepare well for each test.

The second type of testing that homeschoolers consider is GED (General Education Degree) testing. All college applications and financial aid applications require either a high school diploma or its equivalent, a GED.

• My strong advice is: *do not take the GED.* If you are legally homeschooling according to your state's guidelines, and if you feel your son or daughter has earned the equivalent of a high school diploma according to your family's standards, then your son or daughter *has earned a high school diploma* and need not take the GED test. In my opinion, it is most important that homeschoolers avoid having children take the GED. A notation of GED testing, whether on a job application, high school application, or college application, is an immediate "red flag" that tells employers or admissions officers that the student, for whatever reason, dropped out of school. *Homeschooling is not dropping out of school* and we must be ever-vigilant that homeschooled children not be labeled as drop-outs. If financial aid officers, prospective employers or admissions officers question the validity of your homeschooler's diploma, be persistent and remind them that, by law, you are legally entitled to homeschool your child, and therefore, by law, your child has earned a diploma.

You are the expert

As you may have guessed, the most difficult part of the college application process is that *you must become the expert* when your student submits a college application. (If you have homeschooled your child for any length of time, you know you *are the expert,* and indeed you are.) Homeschooling is not something admissions staff commonly encounter. You must learn how to maneuver through their admissions system and show them how your homeschool experience meets their admission requirements.

Here's an example of what I mean: when I tried to get Christian into the University of Wisconsin as a special student at age 16, my first inquiry was met with the response, "We have never had a homeschooling high school student before. We'll have to have a committee meeting to discuss this matter." My next maneuver was to call the University's German department to find out how students are placed in classes. The professor I spoke with said, "All students take a placement test at the University testing office." The test didn't cost anything to take and since the summer semester was about to begin, we decided that Christian should take this language placement test as soon as possible.

University personnel are not used to dealing with round pegs that don't fit into their square holes. Our job was to convince them that our round peg, Christian, was a perfect fit for their square hole. By having Christian take the German placement test early, we were able to include his test score (which qualified him to take a second year honors course) along with letters from two tutors (former graduate students in the German department) with his application. These documents and the application convinced the University admissions staff that Christian should be permitted to take the German classes.

The following year Christian decided to buck the system once again. Even though he was still considered a high school student, he decided that he wanted to take two courses at the University. University policy stated that high school students were only allowed to take one course per semester. As expected, it took more than one phone call to a department, dean or counseling office to unearth the personnel who could be instrumental in getting this rule waived. In my most positive and authoritative voice I asked, "Who can I talk to about getting a homeschooled young man into two classes this fall?" When the rules were quoted to me as the rules governing all "high schoolers," I simply said, "But Christian is not a high school student, so I need to talk to someone who can make a decision based upon his status as a homeschooler." I was told a letter to the Dean of Special Students would be required, and I immediately sat down to compose a letter that briefly described our educational philosophy, Christian's reasons for wanting to attend more than one course, and his previous success taking a five- credit honors course. Again our request was granted and we were told, via a telephone call, that Christian could register for classes on Monday.

Our experience enrolling Georgina in college classes was much easier. When she was fourteen, Georgina decided that she wanted to continue her study of French with a professor who taught at a small Catholic college in town. She was willing to take Georgina in her class and suggested we contact the Department of Continuing Education for admissions information. Continuing Education referred us to the Dean of Admissions. The Dean of Admissions was pleased to admit Georgina based on the professor's recommendation. She could audit the class or take it for credit. Because it would be less expensive, we decided Georgina would audit the class. Because she wanted to do all the assignments, take all the tests and be graded, I asked the professor if this arrangement was acceptable and whether she would be willing to write a letter describing Georgina's progress in the course. She readily agreed. (We ask for such letters for future use for admissions or job applications.)

Since Georgina was only fourteen and this was her first formal classroom experience, she decided to take French 101 even though she'd been studying French for two years. This, she felt, would put her on an even footing with her older, college-age classmates. It also took the pressure off as she learned the routines of college classroom instruction. The experience turned out to be quite pleasant for her and she managed everything — classroom procedures, testing and being graded — quite well.

When Christian was ready to apply for admission to college as a regular student, we considered what we had learned from his first two encounters with admissions offices and proceeded to write our own "prose transcript" describing Christian's achievements. We created a document which included a statement describing Christian's educational experiences, his unique abilities, and our educational philosophy. Separate pages spelled out in detail the specifics of his studies in German, French, English, music, social studies, science, mathematics, and his experiences with volunteer work and employment. For example, we wrote the following description of his science studies:

> One of the philosophies that has guided our homeschooling has been that children are better able to learn when immersed in studies of subjects that have particular interest to them. As a result of our belief in this child-directed, rather than curriculum-directed approach to learning, Christian has not studied the sciences in a traditional manner, but has pursued his own scientific interests. For example, as an eight-year-old he was interested in dissection; we sent away for dissection materials, and he dissected a frog, worm, crayfish, mussel, and fetal pig. Later, as a ten-year-old, he was fascinated with the nature preserve that is at our back door. At that time, he conducted an extensive habitat study of a particular portion of the park. His study included graphing temperature changes, recording numbers of particular species of birds present, and recording and measuring the growth of particular grasses, trees and shrubs. Through this process he became acutely aware of the changes that took place in his habitat. In the following year, his interests shifted to chemistry, and he took chemistry enrichment courses offered through summer programs at the University of Wisconsin and the Madison Public Schools. All of these studies were undertaken because of Christian's interest in the subject matter. His most intense scientific study, though, centered around trout fishing and fly-tying and was carried out over a four-year period.

This descriptive paragraph was followed by a list of specific scientific topics that Christian's study of fishing entailed: entomology, ichthyology, river and lake ecology, physics, and a category we simply called "miscellaneous." Under each of these headings we listed the books and videos Christian had used as resources. In all, we listed over thirty books (none of them traditional textbooks) with titles like *The Trout and the Fly*, by Clark and Goddard; *Trout*, by Schweibert; *Tying Hatch Simulator Flies*, by Swischer and Richards; and *The Essence of Flycasting, Vols. I, II*, by Krieger.

As we thought about how to make this transcript, we realized that we were the only "experts" available. Rather than try to create a traditional-looking transcript, we created a "prose transcript" that we felt best described Christian. This transcript was an educational profile, a description of Christian's homeschooled life. It consisted of material that Christian, David, and I wrote together; copies of Christian's university transcripts; progress letters from his French and German tutors; evaluations sent to us by Christian's counselors and instructors at Concordia Language Villages; employment evaluations; and volunteer job evaluations. We put no grades on this transcript (and didn't include the "report cards" we had used for "Safe Driver" insurance purposes only). The result of our efforts was gratifying; several college admissions officers could see that Christian was college material. (In fact, the Dean of Admissions at Kalamazoo College commented that, "Christian already has a nice portfolio, which is something we want all of our students to prepare before they graduate.") Christian was accepted by his top choice, Kalamazoo College, a small liberal arts school highly ranked for academic excellence, on the merits of his work as documented in our homemade transcript.

One final note about college applications: they all ask for a report from the school counselor and the applicant's class ranking. We had left these lines blank on Christian's applications because we were unsure of what to write. Later on, after Christian had been accepted, I had the opportunity to hear the homeschooling authors, David and Micky Colfax, talk about college admissions procedures. Their advice was to rank our college-bound homeschooled students at the top of their class — because in fact, that is where they are.

Index